# DIARY OF A SMALL HISPANIC COMMUNITY

Juan A. Thomas

**EARLVILLE FREE LIBRARY**
P.O. Box 120
Earlville, NY 13332

Published by the

*The Eugene Paul Nassar Ethnic Heritage Studies Center*

at *Utica College*

Founded in 1981 by Utica College Professor Eugene P. Nassar, the Center serves as a focal point for research, teaching and public service related to ethnicity in American life.

The Ethnic Heritage Studies Committee is responsible for the center's activities. The committee includes:

John Bartle, Ph.D., Russian

Frank Bergmann, Ph.D., English and German (Director Emeritus)

Sherri Cash, Ph.D., History

John Johnsen, Ph.D., Anthropology

James S. Pula, Ph.D., History (Director Emeritus)

Juan A. Thomas, Ph.D., Spanish (Director,

E-Mail: jathomas@utica.edu)

© *2017*
*Utica College*

ISBN 978-0-9660363-2-9

The Eugene Paul Nassar Ethnic Heritage Studies Center
Utica College
1600 Burrstone Road
Utica, N.Y. 13502

Cover Photo: Larry Pacilio "Couple at Mt. Carmel Festival"
© 1975

# Contents

| | |
|---|---|
| Introduction | 5 |
| 1. The Oneida County Hispanic Community | 7 |
|     The Numbers | 7 |
|     Where Are the Hispanics? | 10 |
| 2. The Church Lends a Helping Hand | 13 |
| 3. Hispanics Gain a Voice at LAST | 29 |
| 4. Hispanos Unidos | 49 |
|     Advocacy by Local Newspaper Reporters | 55 |
| 5. The Spanish Language: *Guaguas*, Interpreters, and Language Loss | 61 |
|     Spanish in Health Care: MAMI to the Rescue | 68 |
| 6. The Warrior Symbol | 73 |
| 7. Racial and Ethnic Conflict | 82 |
|     Puerto Ricans versus the Bosnians | 84 |
| 8. Implacable Growth: the 1990s to the Present | 89 |
| 9. Hispanic Representation in Government and Schools | 100 |
|     Hispanics in the Schools | 105 |
| 10. ESL and Educational Achievement | 108 |
|     Educational Achievement | 110 |
| 11. Religion | 115 |
| 12. The Mosaic of Utica's Latino Community | 121 |
|     Chicanos and New Mexicans | 121 |
|     Puerto Ricans | 123 |
|     Dominicans: *Vete al barajo* | 131 |
| 13. A New Association | 138 |
| Epilogue: Work in Progress | 145 |
| Illustrations | 152 |
| Acknowledgments | 155 |
| Notes | 157 |
| Index | 180 |

In Memoriam

Dr. Eugene Paul Nassar

(1935-2017)

# Introduction

In April 2009, Professor Eugene Nassar, founder of the Ethnic Heritage Studies Center at Utica College, and Professor Frank Bergmann, then director of the Center, welcomed me to the Center's committee as the representative of the local Hispanic community. Both of them also urged me to write a monograph about local Hispanics, similar to the chapters that profile eleven groups in the 2002 edition of *Ethnic Utica*.[1] Due to factors beyond their control or wishes, Hispanics were not included in that volume, even though both were very aware that Hispanics form one of the largest and fastest growing ethnic groups in the area.

This book has a local focus, but I hope that those interested in Latino studies will find that it helps to complete the stories about the Hispanic experience in the U.S., because of the particular characteristics of Utica. The decennial 2010 Census revealed many surprises. Even though predictions were confirmed that Hispanics were the fastest growing minority in the country, no one expected such high numbers, as 50.5 million or 16 percent of the total population was Hispanic. Just as surprising, 10.5 percent of Utica's population was Hispanic, and by 2015, estimates pegged the city at 13.6 percent Latino, growing from approximately two percent at the beginning of the 1970s. The increase in the number of Hispanics helped the city to reverse a trend of fifty years of declining population. Paradoxically, this increase has occurred while the area has lost jobs and industries. While large metropolitan areas have traditionally been home to the greatest concentrations of Hispanics, the census showed that recent gains were in rural areas and small cities like Utica. Therefore, this story is an important contribution to the descriptions about the U.S. Latino experience in a type of community that has received little attention in general Latino studies.

This project began as a linguistic study to describe the Spanish spoken in Utica. A language selection questionnaire of 54 Hispanics who lived and worked in Utica showed that Spanish was alive in churches, restaurants and businesses, but, while it was still used in the family, grandchildren typically were English dominant.[2] Longer interviews with 16 of the original 54 participants gave samples of oral Spanish which were analyzed for parameters particularly of interest in the Spanish of the U.S.: subject pronoun expression, possession,[3] the verbal system,[4] code-switching, and Anglicisms.[5] In general, the Spanish spoken in Utica is similar not only to other varieties of U.S. Spanish but also to monolingual varieties found outside of the U.S. The oral samples were also compared to Spanish written in Utica newspapers.[6] Much of the material from the 16 personal interviews and the newspapers has been used as sources for this volume.

The book starts with a review of the census data over time and the locations of Hispanic neighborhoods. The focus shifts to the 1960s-1970s, when the Puerto Rican community began to take on a new prominence in the city. Separate chapters are dedicated to the 1980s and early 1990s as the community continued to grow. Subsequently, a series of chapters focuses on the evolution of specific issues from the 1990s until the present. These include Hispanic representation in the workforce and government, ESL programs and educational achievement, religion, the Spanish language, health care issues, racial and ethnic conflict, and the Mohawk Valley Latino Association (MVLA), a local organization that continues to try to bring the Utica Hispanic community together.

CHAPTER 1

# THE ONEIDA COUNTY HISPANIC COMMUNITY

## THE NUMBERS

The United States Census Bureau uses the labels Hispanic or Latino interchangeably to refer to "a person of Cuban, Mexican, Puerto Rican, South or Central American or other Spanish culture or origin regardless of race."[1] However, members of the major three components of the national Latino community, Mexican Americans, Cuban Americans, and Puerto Ricans, as do all Hispanic nationalities, have different legal relationships with the federal government. Mexican Americans form the largest group of Latinos in the U.S. This group is at the center of the national debate regarding illegal immigration. Cuban Americans have thrived in Florida, and — unlike Mexican Americans — they have, up to very recently, been able to ask for political asylum and relatively quickly acquire citizenship. Puerto Ricans are not immigrants. They are United States citizens.

Even within each of these groups, there is a great degree of diversity. Not all Mexican Americans are native Spanish speakers, as some are speakers of indigenous languages. The first wave of Cuban exiles after the Cuban Revolution and the *Marielitos* of the eighties have very different educational, professional, and racial profiles. Large numbers of Puerto Ricans born in New York consider themselves Nuyoricans. Thus, on the one hand, the U.S. census homogenizes these nationalities together as Latino or Hispanic. Yet, on the other hand, each group has a different legal status as a result of national origin and hence an entirely different set of concerns related to that status. One might suppose that the Spanish language is a common factor among all Latinos and therefore, justifies considering them as one monolithic unit. However, even language can be a source of division.

It is useful to look at the numbers. The 2010 Census counted 50,477,594 Latinos nationwide, or 16.3 percent of the total population. Within the category of Latino, Mexican Americans represented 63 percent of the total, Puerto Ricans 9.2 percent, and Cuban Americans 3.5 percent.[2] The census showed major increases in the Latino population in rural or small urban centers. Although the majority live in the Southwest, the Midwest and the South have seen greater relative increases in numbers of Hispanics. Between the years 2000 and 2010, the Hispanic population in the South and Midwest increased 57 percent and 49 percent respectively, which is four times the total increase in the South's population and twelve times the total increase in the Midwest's population.[3] Although the traditional destinations of Hispanic migration have been large metropolitan areas, the recent growth in the South and Midwest has included rural areas. According to estimates from the American Community survey of 2013,[4] there are 38,417,235 speakers of Spanish in the U.S., making it the second-most spoken language in the country.

Oneida County is a predominately rural county in upstate New York. Utica, the largest city in the county, registered 62,235 inhabitants in 2010. The city is also the fourth largest per capita refugee resettlement area in the country, with refugees from Vietnam, Bosnia, Somalia, Russia, and Myanmar, who make up 15 percent of the city's population.[5] Figure 1 illustrates the growth in the numbers of Latinos in Oneida County as well as the number of Spanish speakers from 1970 to 2015. Over the past half century, as the population of Oneida County has steadily decreased, the number of Latinos has increased, both in absolute and relative numbers, comprising a greater percentage of the population. Based on the American Community estimates for 2015, the percentage of Latinos had risen to 5.47 percent in Oneida County. The increase in the city of Utica has been more pronounced, from 1.1 percent in 1970 to 13.6 percent in 2015. As can be observed, there is a greater number of Hispanics than Spanish speakers. According to the Modern Language Association (MLA), the second-most spoken language in Oneida County has been Spanish since the year 2000.[6]

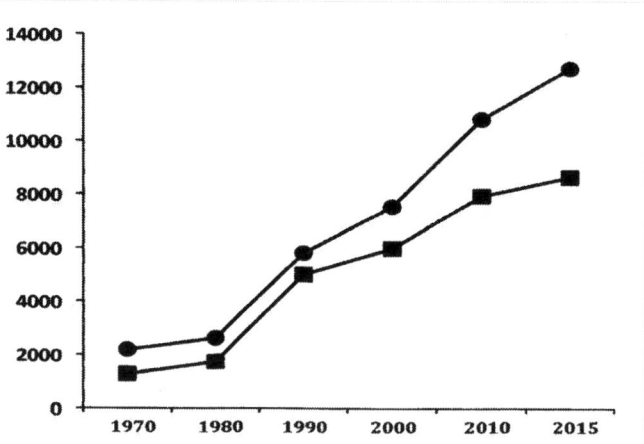

*Figure 1. Number of Latinos (circles) and Spanish-speakers (squares) in Oneida County by year.*

Table 1 indicates that the Puerto Rican group has dominated the Oneida County Latino population throughout the decades. Although Mexican Americans form two-thirds of the national Latino population, 60 percent of Utica's Hispanics are Puerto Rican and 11 percent Dominican. The Puerto Rican dominance in Central New York can be explained by the

| Year | 1970 | 1980 | 1990 | 2000 | 2010 |
|---|---|---|---|---|---|
| Puerto Rican | 607 | 1211 | 3855 | 4883 | 6538 |
| Mexican | 96 | 413 | 472 | 515 | 872 |
| Cuban | 134 | 46 | 81 | 208 | 187 |
| Dominican | - | 1 | 83 | 493 | 1211 |
| Colombian | - | - | 95 | 92 | 109 |
| Ecuadorian | - | - | 28 | 40 | 154 |

*Table 1. Composition of the Latino Community in Oneida County*

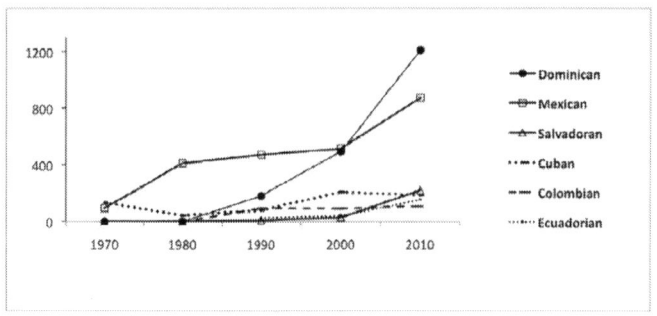

*Figure 2. Number of people by year.*

area's proximity to New York City. Puerto Ricans have long chosen New York City as their destination in the mainland. Figure 2 represents the data in Table 1, without the Puerto Rican count. The Dominican community already had a presence in the county in 2000, but by 2010 they had become the second largest Hispanic group.

## WHERE ARE THE HISPANICS?

Map 1 depicts southeastern Oneida County. The shading corresponds to the percentage of Hispanics as estimated by the five year American Community Survey for 2010-2014; the more darkly shaded the area, the higher the percentage of Hispanics. The uninhabited areas on the map correspond to parks, industrial areas, or airports, with no residential addresses. The two tracts most densely populated by Hispanics in Utica were Tract 208.03 at 23.5 percent Hispanic (662 Hispanics out of 2,820) and Tract 210 at 20.6 percent Hispanic (316 out of 1,532). The other two highest tracts of Hispanic population in Oneida County correspond to prisons. The darkly shaded area in the center of the map is the Marcy Correctional Facility, or Tract 266, which is 26.3 percent Hispanic (788 out of 2,997). Tract 259 has the highest relative number of Hispanics at 29 percent (576 out of 1,782). This is the Mohawk Correctional Facility, located near the city of Rome, the second largest city in the county. As a

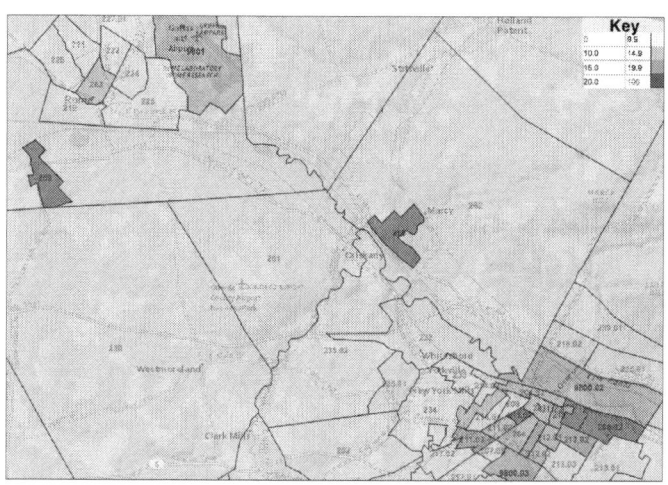

*Map 1. Southeastern Oneida County. Hispanic percentage. 2010-2014 American Community Survey Estimates.*

---

point of reference, the former Griffiss Air Force Base is east of the city of Rome.

Map 2 shows the city of Utica. Bleecker Street in East Utica (running east-west and parallel to the Mohawk River) has been the traditional home to Utica's Hispanic community. East Utica, which is also considered the Italian-American section of Utica, is home to approximately 15 percent of Utica's Hispanics. Although Hispanics are now in all parts of the city, the highest concentrations remain in East Utica. Tracts 208.03 and 210, bordering each other in East Utica, continue to house large numbers of Hispanics. Continuing east along Bleecker Street, tract 208.02 registers 16.2 percent Hispanic. El Barajo Restaurant is on the eastern edge of tract 210, at the corner of Mohawk and Bleecker Streets. Historic Old Saint John's Roman Catholic Church at the corner of John and Bleecker Streets is just off the west end of tract 210, in tract 203 (7.6 percent Hispanic). Off the southwest end of tract 203 is tract 211.03, West Utica, the traditional German and Polish neighborhood. This tract was the third

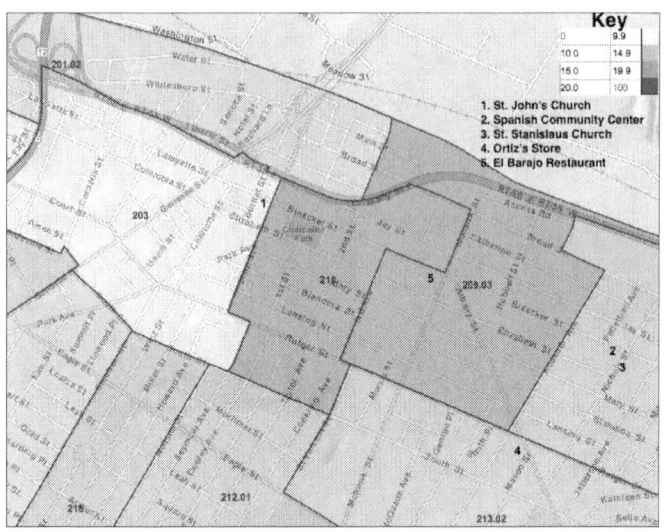

*Map 2. The City of Utica. Hispanic percentage. 2010-2014 American Community Survey Estimates.*

---

most concentrated in Hispanics at 17.8 percent. Off the southeastern edge of tract 203 is the area known as Cornhill, or tract 215, at 15.1 percent Hispanic and over 50 percent black. The Spanish Community Center, which was at 968 Bleecker Street, and Saint Stanislaus Church, around the block from the Center, formed a nucleus of the community especially in the 1970s, along with Santos Molina's store, located in the 900-block of Bleecker Street. Erik Ortiz's store was at the intersection of Kossuth and Albany Streets. Although the maps focus on people declaring themselves of Hispanic/Latino origin, they also reflect the speakers of Spanish. English was not the primary language of all the residents of East Utica and parts of Cornhill. In tract 208.03, over 22 percent were Spanish speakers as per the 2010 Census.

CHAPTER 2

# THE CHURCH LENDS A HELPING HAND

An article in the *Observer-Dispatch (O-D)* cites anecdotal information that the first Puerto Rican was said to have arrived in Utica in 1892.[1] However, substantial numbers of Puerto Ricans did not begin to arrive until the 1940s, searching for jobs, a calmer lifestyle, and a lower cost of living compared to that of New York City. Puerto Ricans found jobs in the textile industry and in the slaughterhouses. The community was centered in East Utica, just as for the earlier Irish and Italian immigrant groups, initially around Saint John's Church. Because of urban renewal in the 1960s, the community became more concentrated eastward in lower Bleecker Street.

Saint John's Church began several outreach programs to help Utica's Spanish-speaking residents.[2] The church offered English classes and catechism classes in Spanish and published a circular in Spanish, *La Voz de San Juan* [The Voice of Saint John], which informed the community of birth, death, and wedding announcements in Spanish. Utica's Hispanic Mission was originally located at the corner of Kossuth Avenue and Bleecker Street in 1956. Masses were celebrated in the Mission and in homes by a Spanish-speaking priest from Saint John's, and later were celebrated in Saint Stanislaus Church.[3]

Saint John's Church, Catholic Charities, and Utica Community Action Inc (UCAi) established the Spanish Community Action Center (often called the Spanish Center) in 1969 at 968 Bleecker Street. Bishop Foery of Syracuse had named Milton Valladares as director of the diocese's Spanish Apostolate Ministry. Valladares, who had come to Syracuse in 1966 from Puerto Rico, was charged with helping the newly arrived Spanish-speaking in areas of health, housing, educa-

*Spanish Action League. From left, Emilio Irizarry, treasurer; Linda Otero, secretary; Alejandro Rivera, vice chairman; Enrique Irizarry Molina, chairman; Milton Valladares, Director Spanish Apostolate.* Observer-Dispatch, *August 10, 1969.*

---

tion, employment, and Christian education. The Diocese of Syracuse paid his salary of $10,500 and named Reverend Theodore Schmitz of St. John's Church his assistant.[4]

Valladares' initial step was to organize the first Hispanic association in Utica, which he called the Spanish Action League.[5] Herman Rivera Zayas, a voluntary worker at UCAi served as league director, at a salary of $5,800. A group of 27 local Hispanics, Valladares, and Father Schmitz met at the Spanish Center on August 5, 1969 and elected officers for the association: Enrique Irizarry Molina, chairman; Alejandro Rivera, vice chairman; Linda Otero, secretary; and Emilio Irizarry, treasurer. Irizarry Molina had also worked for UCAi but left for a better paying job as a butcher at Party Packing Co. The league's first goal was to organize English classes and then religious education, a Christian family movement, and a youth movement, including a chapter of statewide Spanish-speaking youth, whose objective was to encourage youth to attend college.

Valladares spent all of his time in Utica and staffed the Spanish Center along with Sister Theodora of the Daughters of Charity and several volunteers. Sister Theodora had arrived in Utica in October 1969 and had worked for ten years among Bolivia's indigenous population.[6] The center served approximately 125 Puerto Rican families, offering a variety of services such as English classes, income tax preparation, job counseling, mentoring for Puerto Rican boys, and programs for small children.

Susan Tomer profiled the Spanish Community Action Center, Valladares, and Sister Theodora in an article in the *Observer-Dispatch* in February 15, 1970.[7] She told the story of Juan, a Puerto Rican who had been in Utica only a few months with a family of 11 children under the age of 17 and a pregnant wife who was ill in the hospital. Juan, unemployed, had not looked for help, but when Sister Theodora and her high school and college student volunteers missed Juan's children at the after school English lessons, she gathered together her helpers, bought groceries for Juan and his family, and helped to clean the house. Citing Juan's plight as common to that of the city's 1,000 Puerto Ricans, nearly all in the 20-48 age bracket, Tomer pointed out that the Hispanic community faced all the problems of the city's poor, with the added obstacle of a language barrier.

In spite of unemployment or a low wage job, Puerto Rican families valued the educational opportunities available to their children in Utica. Milton Valladares also looked for federal grant opportunities to start an adult educational program. The city's schools cooperated with Spanish-speaking children but were unable to satisfy all the needs, so Sister Theodora's English lessons for elementary school students helped to fill in the gaps. The Utica Police Department announced that police officers would begin to take Spanish lessons to better communicate with the Puerto Ricans, even though few problems with Hispanics had been reported.

In a letter to the editor of the *Observer-Dispatch* on March 7, 1970, Antonia Rodríguez took exception to reporter Susan Tomer's portrayal of the Puerto Rican community.[8] Rodríguez thanked Saint John's Church for offering English language classes and for breaking down the language barrier, one of the biggest problems that affected the Puerto Rican community. She recognized the work done by Sister Theodora and the high school students on the behalf of Puerto Rican children, as well as that by teachers at Wetmore School who had been teaching English as a second language since 1955. Nevertheless, she believed that newly arrived Puerto Ricans were not taking their own initiative to help themselves and that some showed reckless behavior wasting family income on alcohol rather than on necessities. Although Valladares was helping a lot of people, she affirmed that Puerto Ricans who had arrived earlier relied solely on themselves and/or family support and were able to do well. Unemployment was a greater problem in Puerto Rico than in Utica, which explained why many Puerto Ricans continued to migrate to Utica. On the other hand, public assistance benefits for a family of four or more children were higher than a typical salary of $1.75-$2 per hour, suggesting that public assistance took away the incentive to find work. She closed by encouraging Puerto Ricans to learn English and not to expect to use Spanish in Utica.

Regardless of Rodríguez's concerns, Valladares continued to be engaged with the Hispanic community, especially with the youth. He organized a *Fiesta Sunday* on October 11, 1970, with the objective to introduce Utica to its Hispanic community and for the latter to share its culture with the city.[9] Approximately twenty-five members of the teen club prepared for a parade led by local Mexican-American Roque Aguilar. The parade consisted of five floats: the first featured a floral representation of the flags of Puerto Rico and the U.S.A. with Native Americans and explorers; the second represented Columbus; the third showed a horn of plenty; the fourth represented the universe; and the fifth carried the Queen of the Festival along with the flags of Latin America. Events also included a dance and the crowning of the Queen, Hilda Irizarry, by Utica Mayor Dominick Assaro. A three-day festival was held the following year, with Mayor Assaro opening the ceremony,[10] including a *coctel español*, an impromptu Spanish Restaurant set up in East Utica, crowning of the Festival Queen, Spanish and Bolivian music, and a Spanish parade at Oneida Square. That same year, the Hispanic Center's youth also participated in the Sons of Italy Columbus Day Parade.[11] These events helped to enhance the visibility of the Hispanic community in Utica and to involve local leaders.

Valladares quickly became considered the representative and spokesman of the local Hispanic community. He worked to highlight the cultural traditions of the Hispanic community at local events. *Christmas Latin American style* was the theme at Our Saviour Lutheran Church in December 1971, when Spanish Center members presented a program about Christmas customs in Spanish-speaking countries and sang traditional Christmas carols.[12]

Valladares advocated for both Utica's Hispanic and black populations. Mayor Assaro named him and Rev. Theodore to a non-partisan group of citizens to look into the complaints regarding alleged cases of police abuse, following the suspension of a Utica patrolman accused of brutality.[13] In that same year, Valladares led a protest of 25 youths who picketed the Utica School Board because of the Board's decision to replace Gerald Duffy, who had retired, with Miss Marie Russo instead of a black person. Valladares had presented the School Board with a petition of 1,035 signatures, urging the board to select one of six black candidates.[14] In the spring of 1972, two candidates for the Utica School Board, Rev. Franklin Upthegrove and Dr. Edward Cutler, requested endorsement of the local Hispanic community via Valladares' representation.[15] Although Miguel Girona, a Hispanic, had intended to run for the School Board, a misunderstanding prevented him from filing the proper paperwork. Valladares also got involved in a labor dispute between Spaniard Dr. Antonio Gutiérrez Luque and Rome Hospital. Gutiérrez Luque, a neurologist, had been suspended from practicing at Rome Hospital after several complaints about his behavior. Valladares accompanied Gutiérrez Luque to a hearing on September 1, 1971 with the Rome Hospital Board of Managers. The exchange was heated and Valladares was asked to leave.[16]

The Spanish Community Center had been associated with Utica Community Action Inc (UCAi) since its inception. In spite of the difficult relationship between the two organizations, the Center eventually became part of UCAi, changing its name to the East Utica Community Center, with a broad mission to serve all the city's poor. Since his arrival in Utica, Valladares had had disagreements with UCAi, claiming that the organization was a stumbling block for the city's Spanish-speaking citizens because of the lack of a Spanish-speaking representative on the board and the group's refusal to name him deputy director.[17] Since the Spanish Center was considered a multi-ethnic center, Valladares claimed that no programming was directed exclusively at Hispanics. At the inception of the Spanish Center and the Hispanic Action League in 1969, Valladares presented the UCAi with a request of $2,000 to cover the salary of the Spanish Center's director, as well as with a request for $39,202 for a language training program in the 1970 UCAi budget. The UCAi approved the $2,000 salary on September 29, 1969, but it was not until 1972 that UCAi admitted the Hispanic Action League as a delegate agency, with the stipulation that the league would have to seek its own funding from the Federal Office of Equal Opportunity (OEO), and not from the UCAi.[18]

Valladares was charged with a personal foreclosure in 1972[19] and left Utica as quickly as he had arrived, returning to Puerto Rico.[20] William Lagares had become director of the East Utica Community Center by April, 1972.[21] He was also director of youth development at UCAi in 1972 and 1973.[22] Lagares reported on difficulties that first-generation Puerto Rican children faced in the Utica Schools.[23] In the fall of 1971, 269 Spanish-surnamed students were enrolled in the school district, representing 1.9 percent of the total enrollment. Although most were bilingual, Magdalena Santana's story — she was an eighth grader at Brandegee School who had arrived in Utica directly from Puerto Rico — illustrated the difficult experience of a non-English speaking student in the early seventies. Magdalena and her teachers communicated with gestures, sign language, the teacher's limited Spanish, and Magdalena's limited English. Mrs. Penny Schneider, a bilingual teacher, was often called in to help students such as Magdalena when prior attempts to break down the language barrier had failed. Students had usually acquired enough English to function in regular classes by the time they entered high school, according to Miss Gloria Dybas, a high school Spanish teacher. The East Utica Community Center was a place where Spanish-speaking students could practice their English and English-speaking students could practice their Spanish. Lagares summarized other services offered by the East Utica Community Center, including translation, legal interpretation, job referrals, recreational facilities, and the establishment of a high school equivalency degree program in Spanish.

The Center cosponsored five week multi-ethnic summer learning programs. In the third year (1973) 75 students, aged 5-13, participated in the program at Brandegee School.[24] The program was free for all Utica elementary and parochial students. Funding came from a $6,426 federal grant, coordinated by Anthony Scalzo, a Spanish teacher at Proctor High School. The goals were not only to teach English to Spanish-speaking students but also Spanish to English-speaking students. Some students had benefitted from the summer program, such as a girl who had been in Utica for only one week and was rapidly learning English. A monolingual Spanish-speaking boy who had participated in all three summer programs was speaking English as well as anyone else in his school. Students had four hours of lessons per day in physical education, arts and crafts, music, and reading. Instruction was in both Spanish and English by a bilingual teacher, Miss Patricia Gentile, two bilingual teaching assistants, and nine youth workers and included physical education, art, and music. The students went on field trips to Cooperstown's Woodland Museum and Syracuse's Suburban Park.

Frank Calaprice had become director of the East Utica Community Center by April 1975,[25] a job which he would hold for three years.[26] As an employee of UCAi for fourteen years and as a parishioner at Saint John's working with Hispanics, Frank Calaprice "Frankito" became an advocate for the local Hispanic community and one of the most loved by its members.[27] In fact, some people in Puerto Rico were given his name in case they needed any help before arriving in Utica. Calaprice, of Italian descent, became interested in the Spanish language after getting to know some of the first Puerto Ricans in Utica, who had rented an apartment from his father. He studied Spanish at Utica Free Academy High

School and later at Utica College.[28] Calaprice's mastery of Spanish served him well at the East Utica Community Center. He and two other workers interpreted 20 times in Utica courts in 1974 alone.[29] Recognizing the need for Spanish interpretation services, Utica city court judges authorized hiring a Comprehensive Training Act (CETA) certified translator in April 1975.

A dinner was held at Ventura's Restaurant in June 1975 to thank the many volunteers who had helped at the Center.[30] A summary of the awards gives a glimpse of the breadth and scope of activities sponsored by the Center. Calaprice presented certificates to several instructors: Pat Barnum (knitting and crocheting); Maria Beltrametti (pre-school art); Soraida García (bilingual education); Eugene Horton (boxing); Jean Pettigrew and Evelyn Tudhope (Spanish); Ron Hendricks (cardboard carpentry); Anna Perkowski (Polish). Pat Laskovski was thanked for coordinating the Spanish legal documentation workshop; Julio Román Jr. for his work as a commentator on the WKTV's weekly televised Spanish Community Report; and Delia Irizarry, Betsy Carballo, and Lydia Carretero for the Center's tots to teens program. Tony and Norma Irizarry, Alexis and Magda Torres, and Clarissa Cruz were recognized for their compilation of the history of Utica's Puerto Rican community.

As can be seen from above, the East Utica Center offered programs to many people, although its main customers were East Utica Spanish speakers. In the summer of 1975, the East Utica Center joined with the other six Utica community centers in co-sponsoring the annual picnic for Utica's underprivileged children, an event normally hosted by the Cornhill Center.[31] At the beginning of September, the East Utica Center and the Adrean Terrace Opportunity Center co-hosted a Latino Social at Saint John's Church. The 300 attendants danced to a live band, "Sensation Latina" of Syracuse, and enjoyed a buffet of thirty Hispanic dishes.[32] Luis Abrams, a 21-year-old community worker, commented that the recently held social event was a great success, but the $300 necessary to host it would be an obstacle for similar events in the future. However, Calaprice outlined his plans to carry out a census of the area's Hispanics to secure grants for

*Café Tropicano. Playing Dominos. (From left, Juan Morino, Hector Santiago, Santos Molina, Guillermo Lagares.) Photo by Jim Armstrong.* Observer-Dispatch, *October 26, 1975.*

---

federal programs. He estimated the community at 2,000 Spanish speakers, the majority being Puerto Rican.

The 900-block of Bleecker Street was the center of the Spanish-speaking community in the mid-seventies, specifically Santos Molina's Café Tropicano, where Puerto Rican men would gather to play dominoes, and Molina's nearby grocery store, still the only Spanish *bodega* in the entire city.[33] The Spanish language was present everywhere in the 900-block: graffiti, signs, and conversation. The community maintained traditional, male-dominated practices of their native Puerto Rico. Women tended to remain at home, marrying at a young age, taking care of large families, and in many cases not attending high school. Although Puerto Ricans were assimilating to life in Utica, Abrams, who had arrived in Utica from Puerto Rico when he was nine years old, noted that local Puerto Ricans were able to preserve traditions in Utica such as the *parranda*, a Puerto Rican Christ-

*In Santos Molina's bodega. Santos Molina (left) and his son Amanadab (right). Photo by George Widman,* The Daily Press, *April 6, 1978.*

---

mas tradition, where one friend visits another friend, is treated to beverage and food, and then, together, both visit a third friend, sometimes assembling a group of 50 people. The *parranda* was associated with another Christmas tradition, the *posada* [inn], which reenacts Mary and Joseph's (usually portrayed by two local children) search for lodging. Saint John's church had sponsored many *posadas*.

Calaprice and the Center continued to advocate not only for the city's Hispanics but also for all East Uticans. He addressed Mayor Hanna and the Utica Common Council in February 1976, asking for youth centers across the city, more playgrounds, better sidewalks, and more parking spaces to replace demolished homes.[34] The Center's food drive contributed a significant donation to the Emergency Food Bank in December 1976.[35] The Appreciation Night for 1977 honored Reverend John Flanagan, pastor at Saint John's, for his constant dedication to the Center, and Tony Irizarry for his service as president of the East Utica Neighborhood Council.[36] Reverend Flanagan had arrived in Utica in 1973, when masses were being said in homes but were then moved back to Saint Stanislaus. By 1982 the weekly Saturday Spanish mass would return to St. John's. He knew very little about Spanish culture when he took over at Saint John's, but a Cuban nun, Sister Elsa, taught him enough Spanish to say mass. Over the years he would formally study more Spanish, as did his associate, Father Mike Bassano. He felt that the Hispanic Ministry at St. John's kept alive not only a Spanish religious culture but also other traditions, such as the *quinceñera (15 años)* celebration (a type of debutante ball for 15-year-old girls), and the Christmas traditions of the *posada* and *parranda*.[37]

By 1977 there were 400 Puerto Rican families in Utica, roughly 1,500 people, of which 60 percent were unemployed.[38] Two Spanish-speaking teachers worked in the schools: Carmen Miranda, a bilingual kindergarten teacher at Brandegee, and Soraida García, a fourth-grade teacher at Mary Street School. Two Puerto Rican students showed exceptional talent in art: Ralph Ortiz at Proctor and Philip Irizarry at Brandegee. Santos Molina (owner of a grocery store and café on Bleecker Street), Natividad Irizarry (automobile dealer), and Miguel Girona (clothing store owner) were the Puerto Rican businessmen in 1977.

The Hispanic Action League had almost ceased to function by the late 1970s. After Valladares' departure from the area, attempts were made in 1974 and 1976 to revive the group.[39] Non-Hispanics served on the board, and Frank Calaprice, who had become executive secretary of UCAi, called a meeting in February 1978 to reorganize and resuscitate the league. The group met and elected new officers: Miguel Rivera, president; Antonio Irizarry, vice president; Jean Pettigrew, treasurer; Miriam Rivera, corresponding secretary; and Calaprice, recording secretary. Miguel Rivera, husband of Miriam, had arrived in the U.S. in the 1960s and worked as a mechanic for many years before opening up his own business, Miguel's Body Shop. Calaprice articulated one of the many concerns of the 1970s, that not only did local Hispanics have no political representation, they had no spokesman to express their common needs and viewpoints. Non-Hispanics, such as Calaprice, were serving on committees, trying to give a voice to the community. Although many problems were highlighted, such as the lack of Hispanic teachers, discriminatory hiring practices against Hispanics, and lack of Hispanic participation on boards, the group of fifteen members decided to focus its effort on one goal, that of hiring bilingual workers in the Oneida County Social Services Department. The group established regular meetings at the East Utica Community center.

The number of local Hispanics had grown to 2,000 persons by 1978, with 90 percent from Puerto Rico.[40] One of the most well-known Hispanic businessmen of the seventies was Santos Molina. He had arrived in Utica from Puerto Rico in 1948 and owned and operated Utica's only Hispanic grocery store. The store served as a gathering point for Utica's Puerto Ricans, as did his next-door restaurant, Café Tropicano. Molina also rented out apartments.[41] Although he dreamed of returning to Puerto Rico, his son, Amanadab Irizarry, wanted to make his mark in Utica.[42] Molina said that Puerto Ricans continued to move to Utica, 50-60 coming in the beginning months of 1978, in spite of the tight local job and housing market, the language barrier, and the harsh winters. Utica was attractive because of its lower cost of living and less drugs and crime compared to New York City. Utica also had half the unemployment rate that Puerto Rico had. Men tended to secure employment in the slaughterhouses. Puerto Rican women worked outside the home because of necessity rather than by choice, and many found work as seamstresses at Joseph & Feiss or in the Tri-State Laundries.[43] Pat Chamberlain, the director of the East Utica Community Center, explained that the unlucky job seekers tended to move on, resulting in a very mobile population.

Miguel Girona, an outreach worker for Street Time, Inc., an organization that helped ex-convicts adjust to life outside prison, reiterated Santos Molina's wish that most first-generation Puerto Ricans wished to return to the island.[44] Girona was also an announcer for WKTV's Spanish Community Report. Miguel and Rev. Nestor Girona, who were brothers, had opened a clothing store but later moved to Lowville for lower overhead costs.[45]

The Spanish language served to unite Utica's Hispanics, for example when they asked for services in Spanish. On the other hand, Spanish also created conflict within the local Puerto Rican community. Antonia Rodríguez scolded the newer generations of Puerto Rican arrivals for not learning English and demanding services in Spanish. Spanish also segregated Puerto Ricans from the English-speaking members of Utica. Only in the religious context did there seem to be satisfaction with the amount of the Spanish language present. St. John's Church was still ministering to the Spanish speakers of Utica in the late 1970s. Rev. John Flanagan, pastor, and Rev. John Dillon, assistant pastor, both bilingual priests who had worked with the Hispanic community in Rochester, NY, held weekly masses in Spanish at St. Stanislaus Church. The Missionary Church of Christ, a Pentecostal Church, conducted worship services in Spanish with Rev. Nestor Girona, who had arrived in Utica in 1968. He assumed leadership of the church which had existed since 1953 and consisted of a closely knit membership of 50 persons.[46] Girona worked closely with Saint John's, as he felt both were striving to meet the spiritual needs of their members.

The need for more Spanish speakers in the educational and governmental sectors increased throughout the 1970s. According to Mrs. Lorraine Hanley, deputy commissioner for Social Services, even though only 200 out of the 12,000 recipients of public assistance in Oneida County were Hispanic, the need for bilingual Social Service workers was repeatedly emphasized.[47] The Oneida County Social Services department hired the first Spanish-speaking examiner in January 1978.

The Social Services department served Hispanics like Venera Molina, 76. She was Santos Molina's mother and head of the largest Puerto Rican family in Utica. She spent her days preparing large quantities of food for family members who would stop by. Even though she affirmed that she still had *una mente como un reloj* (a mind like a watch),[48] she lived alone and relied on her benefits. She received $257 per month in social security and paid $33 per month for food stamps.

Lack of sufficient presence of the Spanish language in Utica schools was a source of continuous conflict between Hispanics and the local schools.[49] In the latter 1970s, the

Utica School District had some 110-115 Spanish-surnamed pupils. Seventy-five were enrolled in a bilingual program at the Columbus Elementary School, which offered Spanish language instruction in reading and mathematics. The program was originally established in 1969 as a tutorial service at Brandegee School. With the closing of that school in fall 1977, parents were concerned about bussing students to Columbus School, fearing that the dropout rate would increase and that the program would be eliminated. However, their fears did not materialize. The junior high school offered one course in English as a second language (ESL), with 34 Spanish speakers out of the 35 students. The high schools had no established ESL program in the 1970s, although adult classes in English were offered at the East Utica Community Center and at Utica's Career Development Center.

The lack of Spanish-speaking police officers and firemen, as well as allegations of abuse and unfair targeting of Hispanics, were sore spots in the relations between city government and the Hispanic population.[50] Nicolás Irizarry, a father of four and employed at Bendix, had been living in East Utica since 1960.[51] He reported that simple misunderstandings often developed into confrontations between Puerto Ricans and policemen, in part because of the language barrier. Amanadab Irizarry, Nicolas Irizarry's nephew and Santos Molina's son, an army veteran and fluent English speaker, was stopped several times by police during patrols. He believed that the police were deliberately targeting him.[52] He had difficulty finding a job after his discharge, so he enrolled in Mohawk Valley Community College's (MVCC) criminal justice program in hopes of becoming a police officer.[53] Ramón Gómez, who described himself as Mexicarican because of his mixed Mexican/Puerto Rican heritage, a member of the Hispanic Action League, had secured seed money from the United Presbyterian Church for the League. Gómez, an Air Force veteran who had been stationed at Griffiss Airforce Base, graduated from MVCC's criminal justice program and was enrolled as a junior at the State University College of Technology.[54] The mayor at the time, Steven Pawlinga, the police captain, Nicholas LaBella, and the Utica Commissioner of Public Safety, Lewis Kelly, recognized the need for more Spanish-speaking workers (only three Hispanics were on the city's payroll), but they dismissed the charges of police brutality and the deliberate targeting of Spanish speakers.

The East Utica Community Center was one main source of help for many Hispanics in the 1970s. However, toward the end of the decade, Santos Molina and his brother, Nicolás Irizarry, felt that the UCAi was favoring the Cornhill Center while neglecting the East Utica Center.[55] Replying to charges that the Center was denying services to Hispanics and not effectively leading the community, Pat Chamberlain, the Center's director, explained that it was not the Center's responsibility to provide translators for government agencies. The center was staffed at three and Chamberlain was the only one who spoke a little Spanish. Its mission was "to assist people in the community, not to lead them."[56] Local Hispanics should not rely on the Center but rather needed to advocate on their own behalf. Miriam Rivera, corresponding secretary of the newly reorganized Hispanic Action League, speculated that UCAi wished to control the League in order to prevent the East Utica Center from seeking independence, taking along its federal funding with it. Frank Calaprice, former director of the East Utica Community Center and chief promoter of the Hispanic Action League, dismissed Rivera's theories. A longtime supporter and backbone of the Hispanic civic movement, he recognized that many had used the Center as a crutch in the past and that community members took little initiative in organizing themselves. He hoped that the League could effectively represent Hispanics in order to present a united front to articulate Hispanics' needs in a collective manner.

Although community members like Amanadab Irizarry and Nestor Girona remembered Milton Valladares and the sense of awe he instilled in them with his loud, public tirades, no lasting results of his activism remained after he left Utica, and the local Hispanic community continued to be divided and without its own voice.[57] Calaprice penned a letter to the editor of the *Daily Press*, stating that many of the charges against the East Utica Community Center of underserving Utica's Hispanics were levied by people who had never even entered the center. As former director of the Center he averaged 1,400 cases per year, with 95 percent involving Hispanics.[58]

CHAPTER 3

# HISPANICS GAIN A VOICE AT LAST

Nicolás Irizarry went by his father's last name while Santos Molina went by his mother's. The two brothers were among the few Puerto Ricans who had opened up businesses in Utica.[1] In 1980, Irizarry (52) was working at Bendix Corporation. Irizarry first arrived in Utica during a cold winter and was not accustomed to the climate. His brother got him a job at a meatpacking plant, where many Puerto Rican men started because such jobs did not require knowledge of English. He and his wife, Leonor, later prospered and their family grew to five children. Their daughter, Miriam, was married to Miguel Rivera, who owned an auto body repair shop. Rivera (30) came from a large family in Utica of ten brothers and sisters. As head of the Hispanic Action League, he was concerned that the league was having trouble attracting members. The youth were not interested in maintaining traditions, and the older people did not wish to be helped. By living in such small neighborhoods and in large families, the elderly did not have a pressing need to learn English.

In the early 1980s, Irizarry opened the La Palma Restaurant in the 900-block of Bleecker Street. Delia and Hilda, his daughters, worked at the restaurant. Delia was studying at Mohawk Valley Community College and also worked part time at the East Utica Community Center. She commented that womens liberation was not one of the issues in Puerto Rico, because the man was still the boss and girls normally married at age 14 or 15 to have large families. The Utica Puerto Rican community was similar, although girls tended to complete high school and some couples lived together without marrying. Although the job situation in Utica was not favorable, job prospects were fewer in Puerto Rico. Social Service benefits such as welfare, food stamps, and Medicaid were greater in Utica. The unemployed in general did not make problems, although there were burglaries, vandalism, and drug use. Hilda Irizarry, former Hispanic Festival Queen of 1970, felt that the Utica Spanish-speaking community needed to produce professionals; only a few were teachers and none were law enforcement officers. She also wished for a true Spanish Community Center that would be dedicated to preserving Puerto Rican traditions and focusing on the immediate needs of Utica's Puerto Ricans.

La Palma became a gathering point for the Hispanic Community for recreation, especially for popular domino games. Newly arrived people went to La Palma for information about jobs and housing. The East Utica Community Center continued to provide the most help in such matters as job training, English, and information about social service programs. However, unemployment was the biggest problem that Hispanics faced in Utica. Chances improved for job hunters if they knew English, but older members of the community were not taking advantage of English courses that the Utica Board of Education offered at the Center or at the Career Development Center in downtown Utica. Desperate individuals who frequented the La Palma were referred to the East Utica Community Center, which helped them navigate the social services system, although only one Spanish-speaking individual worked at the Oneida County Department of Social Services.

*Miguel Rivera. Photo by Jim Armstrong.* The Observer-Dispatch, *December 21, 1980.*

Armando Zayas, a retired foreman for the telephone company, was a frequent customer of Molina and Irizarry, enjoying the banter and camaraderie in the store's back room. Zayas was patriarch of one of the largest Puerto Rican families in Utica and had helped Santos Molina find a job and an apartment in Utica when he arrived. Molina had prospered. His businesses were centers for the Hispanic community, not only because of the authentic Puerto Rican products he provided from his twice monthly trips to New York City to stock the store but also as a social outlet, where people would gather for talk, drinks, and domino tournaments.

As members of the community continued to emphasize the need for Hispanic police officers and firemen, local politicians tried to recruit more Hispanics into the police and fire departments, but even by 1981 there were no Hispanic policemen or firefighters in Utica or Rome, in spite of efforts by the New York State police, Utica Public Safety Commission, and Utica Police Department.[2] Luis Román of Bleecker Street believed that recruitment efforts failed because Hispanics were not interested in that work and in general had few complaints about treatment by law enforcement officials: "There's a little discrimination here and there, but most Hispanics get a fair shake."[3]

By the he end of 1981, the number of Oneida County Hispanics had reached 2,619 (with 1,230 in Utica). The community was characterized by an approximately 60 percent unemployment rate, limited proficiency in English, and a lack of leadership. As factory jobs became scarcer, some Hispanics tried other careers. Carlos Valladares (43) and his wife, Elvia, opened a grocery store on Bleecker Street after he was laid off from Special Metals. Carlos Valladares was Milton Valladares' brother. Santos Molina continued to run his business, but he had also taken on a job as city bus driver.[4] Opening his own auto body repair shop after working six years at Dodge City was a risky gamble for Miguel Rivera, although the move was worthwhile. He had thought that most of his business would be with the area's Puerto Ricans; however, they only accounted for ten customers per year, and if it hadn't been for non-Hispanics, he would have had to close.[5] Rivera was the former head of the Hispanic-American Action League, which had ceased to meet by 1981. He would often take time off from work to hold meetings, but few people would attend. He attributed the lack of interest to individuals' daily struggle just to survive. An organized group would help to remedy many of the issues that the community faced collectively. The only real representative for Utica's Hispanics was Pat Chamberlain, a non-Hispanic, because of her position as director of the East Utica Community Center. Miguel Girona (30), now working for the post office after having closed the clothing store that he had opened with his brother, agreed with Rivera's assessment that the problems that individual Hispanics faced everyday, such as trying to put food on the table, prevented many from taking part in organizational efforts that would benefit the entire community.[6]

Elving Lagares. Sunday O-D *photo by Mike Doherty.* The Sunday Observer-Dispatch, *December 6, 1981.*

The East Utica Community Center was staffed by Pat Chamberlain; Erin Abrams, secretary; and Milagros Rodríguez, who interpreted. In 1981, the Center received 4,000 calls for help navigating the medical system, nutrition planning, interpreting, counseling, job placement, and legal advice.[7] Eighty percent of those calls came from Hispanics. Rumors spread that federal budget cuts would force the center to close or drastically cut services. Mary Taylor, director of Utica Community Action, assured the community that as of 1981 the center would remain open and in fact, over the past few years, programs such as English as a second language courses and interpreting services had been strengthened.

Elving Lagares (36) put a face on the unemployment problem in 1981, particularly the bleak picture for young, unmarried males among Utica's Puerto Ricans.[8] He had arrived in Utica in 1975, encouraged to come by his brother who was living there. Lagares liked Utica because there was much less crime than in New York City, and discrimination was minimal. Although he was aware of the criticisms di-

32

rected at Utica's schools, he believed that the bilingual and remedial programs met the needs of local Hispanics. He was working part time at the Café Tropicano and interpreting in the courts, as he was a high school graduate and fluent in English and Spanish. The work was sporadic and he was having difficulties making ends meet. Although an unemployed father or mother with dependent children presented a more serious economic problem than an unemployed single male, the latter, in some ways, faced a motivational problem because he lacked children to push him along. Puerto Ricans, especially in Utica, had great hopes for their children. Those hopes inspired mothers and fathers to endure a low-paying job as their children got an education and, in the long term, would have a better life. Hope for the future was not part of the single male's life, and, therefore, some resorted to selling drugs. Lagares thought that a community recreation center might help reduce the temptation for illegal activity.

In spite of the difficult economic times at the end of 1981, the children were finding success. Elliott Rivera, a Proctor High School graduate of 1980, had received a scholarship to Harvard University. Carlos Valladares' son was attending the Riverside School of Aeronautics.

Other Hispanics were actively engaged in their education. Also, the community was united in traditional celebrations. Abraham and Elsa Santiago, who had arrived in Utica in the mid 1960s, and their 11 member family would enjoy a Christmas Eve dinner of traditional dishes, including *pasteles* (a type of vegetable/meat pie), turkey, and various desserts. After dinner, they would celebrate the *parranda*, passing the night singing and playing musical instruments, going door to door to visit friends.[9] Mass also formed a fundamental part of the celebration, along with other parties planned at St. John's Church and the Café Tropicano, where children would break the *piñata*, a papier-mâché figure filled with candy and small gifts. That year, the traditional *La posada* "the inn" was celebrated with José Ramos, 9, and Julia Ortiz, 6,[10] dressed as Joseph and Mary. They were accompanied by 40 people, going from house to house asking for shelter but being denied until reaching the Café Tropicano, where they were allowed in, along with another 60 revellers who had

*La Posada 1981. José Ramos (left) as Joseph. Julia Ortiz (center) as Mary. Photo by Steve Roach.* The Daily Press, *December 21, 1981.*

---

joined them along the way. After a prayer service, the group enjoyed a party. Much of the life of the Hispanic community revolved around religion. St. John's Church had traditionally been the spiritual leader of many local Hispanics. Rev. John Flanagan continued to shepherd Puerto Ricans, as did Rev. Rubén Irizarry of the Missionary Church of Christ and the Rev. José Barrios of the Seventh Day Adventist Church.

The long-feared cuts to UCAi finally occurred in 1982, which resulted in a reduction of $44,500 in federal funding. UCAi had requested $36,000 from the City of Utica's 1982-83 budget but was denied. As a result, offices were consolidated and workers were dismissed, including Milagros Rodríguez and her $7,000 per year job. Rodríguez (25), a native of Ponce, Puerto Rico, had worked for two years as a medical and court interpreter, accompanying Spanish-speaking patients on doctor, hospital, and court visits. She estimated that of the 2,300 Hispanics in Utica, 95 percent were Puerto Rican and 75 percent spoke only Spanish. Although the East Utica Community Center maintained a list of Spanish interpreters, and governmental agencies were acquiring more bilingual workers, government workers often tried to speak Spanish by use of dictionaries. Clients became frustrated because they could not understand. They were more comfortable with Rodríguez because not only did she

*Patricia Chamberlain (left), Angelo Santiago (right). Sunday O-D photo by Mike Doherty. The Sunday* Observer-Dispatch, *December 6, 1981.*

speak the dialect of Spanish that most of Utica's Puerto Ricans spoke, but also as a member of the community she understood their struggles. The loss of her job would be more difficult for the Puerto Ricans that she served than for herself and her family. She had acquired such regard by the Latino community that pregnant women requested her presence when in labor and accident victims asked for her in the ambulance.[11] Pat Chamberlain advocated that as citizens, Puerto Ricans should have access to the services that all citizens can receive, without having to face a language barrier. James Griffin of the UCAi acknowledged the need that Milagros filled, but without $36,000 there was no way that the group could maintain her job. The executive director of UCAi, Mary Taylor, confirmed that the East Utica Center would stay open as long as UCAi existed, but cuts were necessary. Chamberlain was left as the lone outreach worker at the East Utica Center, and the Centers at Gilmore Village and Humphrey Gardens were closed.[12]

Shortly after the announcement of Rodríguez's dismissal, a group of about fifty Hispanics, led by Carlos Valladares and Carmen Santiago, appeared at City Hall on March 23,

1982, demanding a meeting with Utica mayor Steven Pawlinga.[13] Although Rodríguez's dismissal was the immediate issue, it brought to a head a deeply held resentment that the city was ignoring Hispanics. The mayor had spoken at Café Tropicano before the election, promising fifty jobs in the Department of Public Works, the Fire Department, and City Hall, yet nothing had materialized. Pawlinga spoke with the group but said that the issue with Rodríguez's job was a result of President Ronald Reagan's budget cuts rather than a deliberate decision of the city to take away services.[14] Pawlinga pledged to appoint to the Utica Fire Department at least one of the three Hispanic men who were in the process of completing the civil service exam, provided that they showed satisfactory performance.[15] In addition, he set up a meeting between representatives of the Hispanic community and Florio Vitullo, assistant industrial commissioner for the State of New York. The meeting would help the community learn about job opportunities, because at that time the city's finances could not permit any hiring.

The Hispanic community was not satisfied. Charlotte Velez and Carlos Valladares organized a petition drive to keep Rodríguez's job and obtained approximately 500 signatures in less than two weeks.[16] On April 5, 1982, Velez and Luis DeJesús, who delivered the signed petition to City Hall, met with Michael Houseknecht, the city's commissioner of Urban and Economic Development.[17] The group asked the city to devote $13,000 of its Federal Community Development Block Grants to maintain Rodríguez's job. She had been officially laid off the week before the meeting. Houseknecht needed to prepare a budget and present it to the Common Council and to Mayor Steven Pawlinga. The city of Utica did not restore the funding, and by July 1982, UCAi had dismissed a total of 26 staff people, closed three community centers, and ended 17 programs such as the Street Time Recidivism Arrest Program, Community Food and Nutrition, and the Energy Crisis Intervention Program.[18]

One of the long-standing goals of the Hispanic community was realized when Mayor Louis LaPolla appointed the first Hispanic, Amanadab Irizarry (Santos Molina's son), to a provisionary position in the Utica Police Department in December 1983. However, Irizarry was dismissed on June 8, 1984 for unsatisfactory performance.[19] Irizarry believed that he had been unjustifiably let go, only two weeks before he would have graduated from the Utica Police School, claiming that his dismissal was motivated by his Puerto Rican origin. In a complaint to the State Division of Human Rights, he reported that other police officers had told him that he was dismissed because of low grades in police training classes, poor attendance, and an involvement in a bar fight in May 1984.[20] The Utica Police Department would not publicly comment on Irizarry's performance. As a result of the hearing, John W. Walker, regional director of the State Division of Human Rights, dismissed the complaint. The investigation showed that Irizarry was dismissed because his performance as a police officer was not satisfactory and his conduct out of uniform was unbecoming a police officer.[21]

Black and Hispanic leaders denounced the lack of representation of blacks and Hispanics on Oneida county juries.[22] George Sims, who had recently been elected to the Oneida County NAACP, and Rafael Jiménez, organizer of Utica's new Hispanic society, said that this under-representation was preventing blacks and Hispanics from getting an impartial trial. Jiménez attributed part of the problem to the high mobility of Hispanics, who had frequent address changes preventing jury notices from reaching them. Lack of Hispanic representation on juries could hurt Latino defendants because only a Hispanic juror might be aware of cultural differences that could be important in deciding a case.

The Utica Schools adopted some new strategies to increase the hiring of minorities into the school system in 1985.[23] Although minorities in Utica accounted for 8.4 percent of the city's population, almost one quarter of Utica's 9,258 students were minorities. Only 4.6 percent of Utica school district employees were minorities, among whom were no principals or central office administrators. Penny Schneider, an employee of the district for seventeen years and head of the English as a second language program, hoped that she could help her Hispanic students even though she herself wasn't Hispanic. Jeanne Arcuri, School Board Vice President, thought that the district already had fair hiring practices. School Board member David Mathis, however, explained that he never had a minority teacher during his years as a student in the system in the 1950s and 1960s. Studies showed that integration enhances all students' experiences by their interacting with different people. The hiring practices in Utica schools, which favored relatives of school board members or administrators, increased public skepticism of the integrity of the process.

In addition to the low presence of Hispanics in the school system, the need for Spanish language interpreters continued to be stressed in the mid-1980s, especially in the medical and social service areas.[24] Frank Calaprice continued to help with interpretation cases even though that was not part of his job. Members of the community such as Elecuterio Torres, a disabled, unemployed father of three, had forged friendships with Calaprice because of the voluntary help he offered. Torres had been in Utica for two months when he called Calaprice for help with his mentally handicapped sixteen-year-old son as well as for help with Social Security and welfare benefits. The fact that Hispanics usually stopped seeking services when the language barrier arose or brought along their own interpreter often masked the problem to medical and social service officials, who reported little difficulty in communicating with Utica's non-English-speakers. Hispanics who did not have complete mastery of English made sure that they sought services with someone who spoke English, usually a child who should have been in school. Gladys Román, who had lived

*UCAi Headstart Program. José Rosado(left). Frank Calaprice (right). Photo by George Widman. The Observer-Dispatch, December 21, 1980.*

12 years in Utica with her husband Dionisio, felt that her English was good enough, but when she took her 11-year-old son Deane to the hospital because of pneumonia, nobody could understand her. She returned home with the child and did not go back to the hospital.

From the perspective of the social services organizations, Raymond Schultz, district manager of Social Security, and Allan Pollicove, director of the Oneida County office of income maintenance (which determined eligibility for food stamps, health programs and public assistance), believed that their offices did not need to provide interpretation services or hire bilingual workers since they had pamphlets and forms published in Spanish. They had a few employees who spoke Spanish, but most Hispanics who used their services were accompanied by family members.[25] Utica City Judge Anthony Garramone and Oneida County Judge John Buckley said that they were able to hire interpreters, but in six years, Buckley only needed an interpreter in ten cases. St. Elizabeth's, Faxton, and St. Luke's Memorial Hospitals maintained lists of bilingual staff who were available for interpretation.

In the mid-1980s, the closings, downsizings, or relocations of companies such as GE, Beaunit Mills, Utica Radiator, and Sperry Univac resulted in 90 to 95 percent unemployment of people who had had manufacturing jobs, according to Pat Chamberlain who continued as director of the East Utica Center.[26] Two of the three former slaughterhouses had also closed. More and more Hispanics were trying to start their own businesses. Nelson Santiago had started his own business, The Last Tangle Salon. However, very few Hispanic businesses in Utica succeeded because of lack of experience. In 1985 the longest-running Hispanic business was Miguel Rivera's auto body repair shop, which had been open for nearly a decade. Many Hispanics started businesses with their own capital investment, rather than bank loans, because of lack of experience with banks.

Lack of business experience in such fundamental matters as choosing a good location set the new business owner up for failure. Even Santos Molina's grocery store on Bleecker Street, which had been an icon in East Utica for twenty-five years, had closed. Molina was driving a Utica Transit Authority bus. His wife Elsa and nephew Sebastian Torres (31) were renovating an old building on Bleecker Street with the goal to open a Spanish supermarket.[27] Torres was glad for the work since he was unemployed and had sought help through Manpower, getting jobs in car repair and construction, but with no permanent position. Gregorio Picart, married to Nelson Santiago's sister Carmen, bought the Café La Palma from Nick Irizarry in October 1984. Picart had worked as a machinist for twelve years at Bossert Manufacturing Co. until the company declared bankruptcy and closed. Business was slow, but Picart kept Irizarry's schedule of opening in the evenings and weekends. Jeff Ortiz (20), a recent graduate of Proctor High School, opened a novelty shop on Bleecker Street. Ortiz had travelled to Georgia in search of work but returned to Utica. His rent was low, and he provided products such as tee shirts and soft drinks. He named his store "Adjuntas" since it was "next door" to the tavern Café Flamboyan run by Michael Chaparro, who had lived in Utica off and on since 1967. Chaparro had been in New York City, but on returning to Utica to visit relatives, he felt something new in the air, in spite of all the factory closings. Hispanic professionals, other than Puerto Ricans, were arriving in the area. Rafael Jiménez, vice president of LAST, believed that Hispanic businesses were poised for success because of the growing population of Latinos, not only in Utica but also in the entire country.

A new group of leaders from the Hispanic community, including some members of the former Hispanic Action League such as Miguel Rivera, decided to form a new organization in February 1984.[28] The community had seen few changes even after their brief unification when trying to save Rodríguez's job.[29] There were no Hispanics in the fire and police departments and only a few Hispanic teachers. Younger people were turning away from the Spanish language and Puerto Rican culture, wishing to adopt the U.S. lifestyle. Older people, on the other hand, preferred to live in a close-knit but isolated community centered in Bleecker Street around the East Utica Community Center, La Palma, the Café Tropicano, and Santos Molina's grocery store. Even

*Rafael Jiménez (left), Nelson Santiago (right). Photo by* Observer-Dispatch, *June 16, 1985.*

though the Utica Hispanic population had doubled from 1970 to 1980, there was no active Latino association. The president of the new organization, Latin American Society for Togetherness (LAST), was Nelson Santiago, and the vice president was Rafael Jiménez, a pharmaceutical salesman. Nelson Santiago (28) was born in Puerto Rico but had arrived in Utica when he was in third grade. He grew up in the 900-block of Bleecker Street, the heart of Utica's Puerto Rican community. His father, Abraham, a former Utica Radiator employee, and his mother, Hilda, strongly emphasized education. Nelson was the second oldest of eleven brothers and sisters, most of whom had been educated in Utica and now were working at many different jobs, including at GE and in civil service and hospital settings. Santiago had been running two hair salons for two years.[30] By the mid-1980s, LAST, especially via Rafael Jiménez, had become the *de facto* spokesman for the Utica Hispanic community.

Jiménez was concerned about the divisions in Utica's Hispanic community. The first group consisted of Puerto

*LAST helps Puerto Rico. From left, Rafael Jimenez, Luis Montero, Carmen Colón, Miguel Rivera. Photo by Mike Doherty*, The Sunday Observer-Dispatch, *November 6, 1985.*

---

Ricans who came to East Utica in the 1950s. They settled for low-paying jobs and tended not to learn English. The second group was a younger group, many born and educated in Utica, who spoke English and had attended college. The second group also consisted of other college-educated Hispanics from Mexico, Cuba, and other Latin American countries, who had made their lives in Utica. Jiménez (31 years old in 1985) had attended Amherst College in Massachusetts and counted himself among the second group. He, his wife Mercedes, and their two children had arrived in Utica in 1982 to make their home in New Hartford. Jiménez was proud of his heritage and wished to preserve it, and he also wished to dispel the many stereotypes that Hispanics faced. Rev. John Flanagan thought that LAST could help unify the community. As pastor of Saint John's, he wasn't sure why the community had not unified. Miguel Rivera thought that the new organization was off to a good start, but more needed to be done to realize LAST's goals.[31]

LAST wished to unify the Hispanic community, promote understanding of Hispanic culture, and break negative stereotypes of Hispanics. The group planned initiatives such as a voter registration drive, community lectures, a newsletter, and a summer cultural festival and marathon. The *Baile de San Valentín* (Saint Valentine's Day Dance), held on February 11, 1984, was its first event. The group was designated as a non-profit and relied on fundraisers to support itself. An editorial in the *Observer-Dispatch* lamented the fragmentation within Utica's Hispanic community, considering it small and powerless, lacking political clout because of language preferences, attitudes, and perceptions. The editor hoped that LAST would be able to unite the community, as earlier immigrant communities had been united in Utica, in order promote their own self interest.[32]

The leaders of LAST understood the importance of education in their lives, as did many members of Utica's Hispanic Community. Dr. Roberto Ross, originally from Mexico, was performing a three-year internship in the emergency ward at St Elizabeth's Hospital. Although he could not participate in LAST as much as he would have liked, he believed that the association was a valuable tool to foster unity in the Hispanic community. Ross stated, "Ethnic groups should get together to help each other in finding jobs and getting an education. Education is the key in all this; only education can point the way to the better future we all want."[33] Both Nelson Santiago, president of LAST, and Dr. Ross dealt with many Hispanics in their respective jobs, and both believed that people want to understand and be understood. They felt that it was important that they spoke both Spanish and English in order to help all their customers and patients. LAST strove to educate Hispanics in the benefits of unity, noting that the older members of the community, living in Spanish, were separated from the mainstream English-speaking community. Santiago and Rafael Jiménez wished to start a social movement that would bring the community together. By mid-1985, LAST had held dances, a "Miss Latin Utica" contest, and a "Latin Mother of the Year" contest.

In order to celebrate a Hispanic Heritage Festival (last held by Milton Valladares in the early 1970s), LAST was trying to raise about $4,000 but as of August 1985 had only $1,500.[34] The group directed a letter-writing campaign to

Utica business leaders, appealing for funds. The festival was held on September 15 at Saint John's Church, with an estimated attendance of 1,000, twice the number expected. Attendees enjoyed music by El Combo Latino from Syracuse as well as traditional arts and crafts, baked goods, and a cookbook made of recipes from the community. The contestants for the Miss Hispanic Utica honor also were presented. Although music, games, and food were a main part of the celebration, perhaps the most important part was the voter registration drive, which registered fifty Uticans to vote.[35] LAST aimed to enhance the social and political visibility of Utica Hispanics, which could not be done without more voting by Hispanics. Money raised at the festival was to be used to purchase the Ukrainian Hall on Bleecker Street in order to build a center for meetings and to have space for a library, gymnasium, and activity rooms. The group wished to open a chapter at Griffiss Air Force Base in order to facilitate membership for Hispanic airmen.

In spite of its goal to foster unity, LAST was a source of conflict. Robert Ramos had organized the "Miss Latin Utica" contest in 1983. In the following years, LAST wished to convert the pageant into a fund-raising effort and decided to award the title to the candidate who raised the most money by selling votes for herself. Ramos, a professional singer and dancer who had moved to Brooklyn, objected to that procedure, saying that it ignored the values that were originally established for the pageant. Contestants would be judged by a panel on beauty, verbal ability, poise, presentation, dance, and appearance. Since Ramos owned the rights to the title "Miss Latin Utica," LAST would award a new title, "Miss Hispanic Utica," in order to avoid a legal battle.[36] Linda Irizarry, a senior at Proctor High School and daughter of Nicolás and Leonor Irizarry, was crowned "Miss Hispanic Utica" of 1985. She had collected $1,501, selling votes at twenty-five cents each, and would represent LAST at various events, including the Columbus Day parade at the Sons of Italy. Linda's older sister, Hilda Irizarry Santiago, "Hispanic Festival Queen" of 1970, was on hand for the presentation at St. Francis DeSales School. She had also been chosen by selling votes, fifteen years earlier.[37] The other contestants,

*La Posada 1980. Virgen Molina (left) Steve Garcia (right). Photo by Kay Arcuri,* The Observer-Dispatch, *December 21, 1980.*

Elisa Maria Cortes, Maria Maldonado, Virgen Molina, Oneida Miranda, Debbie Wilmore and Marian Pagan, said that they were happy to contribute to LAST's goal of raising $100,000 to establish a community center. The "Miss Hispanic Utica" 1986 title went to Elisa Maria Cortes (17), a freshman at MVCC. The coronation award was a trip to Puerto Rico and $100 spending money.[38] Each of five contestants gathered her own votes at one dollar each.

LAST also tried to cultivate a spirit of solidarity with Puerto Rico with its drive to aid the victims of flooding in October 1985. The majority of the association's members came from Ponce, Puerto Rico, one of the affected areas.[39] Over 60 people were killed in a tropical deluge that triggered floods and mudslides.[40] Miguel Rivera and Nelson Santiago, who both had relatives in Ponce, said that their family members were safe but that other area Puerto Ricans had not yet made contact with their families.[41] The appeal raised $1,000 and collected 70 cartons of clothes. Owing to the long-time support that Historic Old St. John's Church had maintained with Utica's Hispanic community, the Church contributed financially to the appeal and served as a collection point for the drive.

In 1985, Mario Colón (32), Puerto Rican born and Utica resident since the 1960s, presented his candidacy for the Utica Common Council, 5th District Seat, Cornhill, running on the "New Media Party" and hoping to be the first Hispanic councilman of Utica. Colón was employed as a teacher in the Utica School system and also as an insurance salesman. However, amid an election year full of controversy, Colón received only 43 votes.[42] He attributed the poor result to the obscure area where his name had been placed on the ballot. On weighing in on Colón's defeat, Rafael Jiménez said that Colón was not a member of LAST and had not been endorsed by the organization. Even though one of LAST's goals was to elect a Hispanic to the Utica Common Council, Jiménez felt that the timing was not right and that the organization would not endorse a candidate because he or she was Hispanic.[43] Pat Chamberlain was surprised at the low vote count because Colón had undertaken an aggressive door-to-door campaign. She speculated that perhaps if he had run in the East Utica Ward he might have had more success as that area was the heart of the Utica Hispanic community where approximately 2,500 Hispanics lived. Cornhill had approximately 300 Hispanics.[44] Colón planned to run for the 116th Assembly District in 1986. However, he withdrew and endorsed Utica Councilman Louis Critelli, D-6. Colón and his wife Luisa were expecting their second child and he could not devote the time needed for the job.[45]

The second Latin Festival, "Carnaval Latino 1986," was integrated into the "Good Old Summertime" series.[46] Senator James Donovan, R-47, obtained a $2,500 grant to help underwrite the costs of the festival, held on July 12-13, 1986, at Historic Old Saint John's Church. The two-day event was chaired by Rafael Jiménez and beauty queen Linda Irizarry and included three bands, a male and female beauty contest, and dancing. LAST represented the Hispanic community at the Holiday of Nations celebration held in November 1986.

Saint John's Church helped to keep not only Christmas traditions alive in the local Hispanic community but also the very important celebrations of Holy Week, specifically the Good Friday procession and *Via crucis*.[47] Rafael Jiménez and his wife Mercedes explained that Good Friday — not Easter Sunday — was traditionally the big day of religious observance in their native Puerto Rico. The day was designated as a fasting day with only a light breakfast and supper, called *verdura* (vegetables, greens), in Jiménez's household, because meat was avoided. Music and dancing were also prohibited on Good Friday. *Sábado de Gloria* (Holy Saturday) was a day for celebrations. The Easter bunny and egg decorating are not traditions in Puerto Rico but instead weaving crosses from palms. Saint Johns marked the occasion with a special service and a procession inside the church, while in Puerto Rico, the Good Friday procession would be outside.

As part of the National Hispanic Month Celebration, LAST hosted a dinner in September 1989 at St. John's Parish in order to honor some local Uticans.[48] Luis Sotomayor, a new resident to the community, was honored for rescuing children from a Mortimer Street fire in August. Sotomayor (37) had arrived in Utica on June 24, 1989 from Juyuya, in central Puerto Rico.[49] He had worked there as a policeman but moved to Utica on the urging of his good friends, Alberto and Emma Meléndez, who had arrived in 1988. Sotomayor, his wife, Elizabeth, and their three children left all that they had in Puerto Rico, convinced that a better life awaited them in Utica, even though he and his wife had difficulty finding work. His eldest son and daughter could not walk. They attended special daily classes in the Utica School District. This service was a great advantage compared to their situation in Puerto Rico, where they were homebound and instruction was limited to once per week. Luis and his wife said that they did not care about the difficulties they were facing because the quality of their children's lives was much better in Utica than in Puerto Rico.

The Forum "*Somos Uno*: A Regional Conference on Hispanic Affairs," held in Utica in September 1989 at the Neighborhood Center, highlighted the success of some Hispanics such as Joseph Fernández, newly appointed chancellor of the New York City Schools. Sixty percent of 3,000 Hispanics who had attended a similar conference earlier in 1989 in Albany had family incomes of $50,000 or more, half held bachelor's degrees, and all were registered to vote.[50] Yet the 70 representatives of various civic, social, governmental, and educational agencies who attended the Utica conference heard more about the problems that many Hispanics faced, such as babies born with AIDS, high incarceration rates, poverty among the elderly, and a high educational throwaway rate. The latter referred to the fact that Hispanic students were not dropping out but, rather, the system was throwing them away. In reacting to the conference, various local Hispanics articulated what they thought the community needed. José Belmar, a caseworker with the Oneida County Department of Social Services, expressed the need for a centralized agency to provide services for Hispanics. Hilda Santiago, the director of the East Utica Opportunity Center, said that the current center did not have enough space to meet the needs of educational and training programs. Michael Tirado, program director for the Utica Community Action group, also reiterated the need for better access to services and more Hispanic caseworkers.

Chapter 4

# HISPANOS UNIDOS

Michael Tirado, a member of LAST and the New York State Hispanic Task Force, became the first Hispanic to serve on a major city commission at the beginning of the decade of the 1990s.[1] Citing Tirado as someone who really cared for the community, Mayor Louis LaPolla named him to fill a vacancy on the five-member Utica Auditorium Commission. Tirado was appointed to complete Jerry Gilberti's five-year term (Gilberti had moved from the area).

Nevertheless, Hispanics remained underrepresented in educational settings. Only 21 minorities were among the 663 teachers employed by the Utica School District in 1992. Mercedes Rivera, Rafael Jiménez's wife, an English as a second language (ESL) teacher in Wetmore Elementary school, expressed her philosophy, stressing that part of her job was to increase children's self-esteem. She was 20 years old when she arrived in the U.S. from Puerto Rico and had an immediate desire to work with children. She had taken classes at the University of Connecticut but had had difficulty with her coursework. She transferred to the University of Massachusetts and finished her courses at Utica College after her family had moved to Utica. Based on her personal experiences, she understood the special problems that monolingual non-English speaking children faced. They needed role models. She worked not only with Spanish-speaking children but also with students from Cambodia, Vietnam, and Laos. She believed that if more teachers had learned a foreign language, they would better understand the struggles of their ESL students.[2]

One of Rafael Jiménez's last projects in Utica made use of his entrepreneurial expertise. He had grown up in a family working in the restaurant business in Puerto Rico. Given that the number of Hispanics locally and nationally continued to increase and that they tended to spend considerable amounts of money on food, he thought that a traditional product would be marketable. Working together with José Santiago at Dino's Sausage in Utica, they developed and marketed *longaniza*, a type of sausage. The sausage was featured at the 1992 New York State Christopher Columbus Quincentenary "Picnic on the Pier" celebration in New York City. Santiago's and Jiménez's company, called "Mercedes" for Jiménez's wife, was the only upstate business represented at that function.[3] Rafael Jiménez remained in the area. He had left his job in pharmaceutical sales to start a restaurant, Mambo's, specializing in low-fat, low-cholesterol, and low-sodium Caribbean cuisine.[4] Because of financial problems, he closed the restaurant in June 1995 and a few years later relocated to the west coast, returning to pharmaceutical sales.

Reacting to the fast growth in numbers of local Hispanics but the lack of services and representation, Anna Irizarry Zayas, Marilyn DeSuárez, and Sofia Novoa formed "Hispanos Unidos" (United Hispanics) in October 1992.[5] They emphasized that the language barrier continued to be the main problem, which resulted in survival issues for many local Hispanics. The mission statement of Hispanos Unidos was "The unity and progress of the Hispanic community" and was intended to be as open-ended as possible.[6] This group administered surveys, held conferences, and wrote columns in Spanish for the local newspaper, *The Observer-Dispatch*.

Marilyn DeSuárez was the eldest child of Gladys and Emilio Irizarry. The Irizarry family was one of the largest Puerto Rican families in Utica.[7] Emilio Irizarry had served on the board of the Hispanic Action League, founded by Valladares. Members of the family had been active participants in the life of the Utica Hispanic community for many years. Gladys and Emilio Irizarry, both originally from Puerto Rico, were raising their 11 children in Utica on Lafayette Street. Their large family filled their lives with joys and problems. Emilio worked as an auto mechanic, and Gladys cared for the family. They had not planned to have such a large family but were pleased with their many children. While they didn't recommend a large family for everyone, they believed that the size depends on what the parents can manage. In all situ-

*Hispanos Unidos. Marilyn DeSuarez (left), Sofia Novoa (right) Photo by Gary Fountain,* Observer-Dispatch, *November 5, 1992.*

---

ations though, the family must be close and maintain open communication before issues become problems. DeSuárez believed that the advantages of a big family outweighed the disadvantages, although her parents, especially her mother, sacrificed her own needs to provide for the children.

The Oneida/Herkimer Human Needs Assessment Survey (O/HHNA) was administered in 1990. That survey did not ask about services needed in Spanish. Also, only an English version was prepared. One of the first contributions of the new Latino association was the Hispanos Unidos Needs Assessment (HUNA), tailored to the Hispanic community. Surveys were prepared in both English and Spanish and were available in Hispanic businesses, restaurants, clubs, and various social agencies in 1993. A total of 104 surveys were completed. The results were released in 1994.[8] The HUNA showed that Hispanics had at least a 20 percent greater need than the population surveyed in the O/HHNA in terms of work, housing, and medical care. More than 38 percent had difficulties paying their rent and utilities. HUNA also showed that many Hispanics in need did not seek help: 22

percent because they didn't know where to go, and 15 percent because services were not available in Spanish. Only 56 percent of the Latino residents who were U.S. citizens were registered to vote, and only 24 percent of Hispanic women who spoke only or mostly Spanish were registered to vote. Local Hispanics used Spanish considerably in the 1990s. The vast majority (82 percent) cited that the lack of services in Spanish was a problem.

The low number of Hispanics registered to vote locally correlated with national trends even ten years after the Hispanos Unidos survey. Hispanics, especially those with limited English ability, wished to become American citizens but were not sure how to initiate the process, often paying large sums of money to unscrupulous individuals to help them.[9] In 2001, only a very few minority candidates were on the ballot locally, even though by the Census of 2000, ten percent of Oneida County and 20 percent of Utica were minorities.[10] Minority candidates were in races where a majority of minorities lived. Fran Williams, head of the Oneida County Branch of the NAACP, wished to see more minority candidates. The key was to increase voter registration in the minority dominant districts, such as Cornhill, as well as voter education. William Hendricks, though, running for reelection as Oneida County legislator, did not wish to be considered a minority candidate but rather a candidate.

The decade of the 1990s also saw the expansion of the Spanish language in the local media. Sergio Espinal, a Dominican who arrived in the Utica area in the early 1980s, and Carlos Manuel De La Rosa started a weekly radio program in 1991, *Con sabor latino en sábado contigo* (With Latin flavor on Saturday with you). When De La Rosa arrived in the mid-1980s, stationed at Griffiss Air Force Base, he felt cultural isolation, which prompted trips to New York City just to listen to his favorite music. He hoped that nobody would have to go through what he did, so he started the program, which also aimed to celebrate 500 years of Hispanic culture in the Americas, to contribute to the maintenance of Hispanic culture, and to help foster a sense of community among local Hispanics. Hispanic ballads, salsa, and merengue dance music were featured. The program was well received. A letter-writing campaign sponsored by area Hispanic businesses generated about 100 requests asking the radio station to increase the show to three hours per week.[11] Hamilton College and Utica College Latino social clubs also supported the show.[12] Besides the radio program, the *Observer-Dispatch* began to feature in 1993 a bi-monthly column *El Despertar Hispano-Americano/Hispanic-America Awakening*, written in Spanish and translated into English.[13] The column highlighted the positive contributions of local Latinos. Most topics related to the local area; others of a more general scope, dealt with the Latino experience in the United States. Some columns were of general information such as the history of chocolate,[14] and others were political in nature, related to the plebiscite in Puerto Rico regarding statehood, independence, or the continued *estado libre associado* status.[15]

Columns related to topics of general interest to U.S. Hispanics included: keeping Spanish in the family or not,[16] the role of teachers in their children's lives,[17] the concerns of Latino mothers about corrupting influences on their children.[18] Not only unfulfilled dreams but a turn toward delinquency worried many Hispanics.[19] For example, one column told the story of Toño, who left his island home, promising his grandmother that he would return from the United States as a doctor. However, he changed on the mainland, and not only did he not fulfill his promises to his grandmother but he landed in jail. The story of Toño was fictionalized but yet typical. One out of ten Latino men in their twenties was in jail or on parole, many because of drugs. Only ten percent typically completed high school, and 40 percent were illiterate. The drug problem preyed especially on Hispanics both in the United States and in Latin America, tricking them with false promises to free them of their troubles.[20]

Discrimination and prejudice challenged Hispanics in ways that marked their future lives and happiness. Josefina Bonilla-Grasso of Rome told of her personal experience with discrimination and bullying she faced as a young girl growing up in Boston.[21] As one of only three minority students among the thousands of white students at Boston Latin, the name calling and prejudicial attitudes motivated her to lose her Spanish accent. However, in high school, her Latino

*Clippings from El Despertar hispano americano, The Observer-Dispatch, 1993-1994.*

---

brothers and sisters also were unwilling to accept her. She struggled with two identities and realized that prejudice goes two ways. As an adult she has tried to work against these prejudices in her daily interactions with people.

Salvador Pérez attended the sixth annual New York State Assembly Puerto Rican Hispanic Task Force's conference in Albany, *Rompiendo Barreras-un reto al cambio*. The goals of the statewide conference were to provide information on Puerto Rican/Hispanic community issues, to recommend budgetary items and executive actions to address social and economic problems with the community, to improve services to the community, and to evaluate the effectiveness of current programs.[22] Assemblywoman RoAnn Destito from the 116th District pledged support for the agenda as well as support in convening a similar conference for the local area, which eventually culminated in *Rompiendo Barreras Culturales — Breaking Cultural Barriers* held on October 29, 1993, at the Cosmopolitan Center. A steering committee consisting of Marilyn DeSuárez of Hispanos

Unidos, Elizabeth Spraker of the ACCESS Center of Oneida County BOCES, Esteban Espinal, Luis Cardona, Frank Calaprice, and Henry Marshall organized the conference.[23] Topics included employment, housing, accessibility to services and education, especially ESL classes and basic educational services. These topics were considered crucial for Latinos who wished to enter mainstream American life and to participate in democracy. Assemblywoman RoAnn Destito's office coordinated the activities of the steering committee, which established the agenda. The conference was considered a historic and productive meeting in the local Hispanic community[24] in spite of the "heated exchange of convictions."[25] Even though the statistics showed that Hispanics needed help, many preferred to rely on themselves instead of asking for government handouts.

## ADVOCACY BY LOCAL NEWSPAPER REPORTERS

Besides the *Despertar Hispano-Americano* columns in the *Observer-Dispatch*, several reporters, especially Tim Chavez and Jorge Hernández, advocated in behalf of the local Hispanic community and brought forth issues of local and national relevance to the readership of the paper.

By 1998, Hispanics were leaving school at a rate almost triple the national average. Close to twenty percent of Hispanics in the 16 to 24 age group who ever had enrolled dropped out. Tim Chavez cited factors other than language skills: lack of teachers with appropriate training, lowered academic expectations, and school bureaucracies that did not encourage involvement of parents.[26] Chavez wrote of a Catholic School in Palo Alto, California. In an area of high poverty and high violence, with a student population of 62 percent Hispanic and 22 percent black, not only did students complete high school, nearly two thirds entered college. Most Hispanic students spoke Spanish at home, and some parents knew very little English. The school's secret was to provide a bilingual environment whenever possible. School notices went out in English and Spanish, the school's secretary was bilingual and there were four Spanish-speaking teachers. Perhaps the most important difference was parental involvement. All parents had to serve the school in some capacity, whether on the school board, helping with lunches, construction, and so on.

Tim Chavez, one of the leaders of the local Hispanic community in the 1990s, left his job as the *Observer-Dispatch* Opinion Page editor in September 1996 to become a columnist for the *Nashville Tennessean*.[27] Before he left, he was honored with the "First Annual Interfaith Bridge Builder's Achievement Award" for his efforts to build bridges of understanding to end racism in the community. His columns and meetings eventually led to the formation of the Interfaith Bridge Builders Coalition. He was an outspoken defender of civil rights and denounced the racism he saw in many community conflicts. Professionally, he was among the 15 editors nationwide who were honored by Gannett Newspapers for improving their newspapers and serving the community. In 1994, he won a Gannett Award as top columnist. His writings, from contributions to *El Despertar Hispano Americano* to his weekly columns, highlighted Hispanic issues on both a local and national level.

Although Tim Chavez had left the Utica area, he continued to publish columns in the *O-D* which dealt with Hispanic issues. Society's ignorance of Hispanic issues was evident even by the lack of interest in Hispanic Heritage Month. President Lyndon Johnson first declared a week in September 1968 National Hispanic Heritage Week. It wasn't until 1988 that it became a Hispanic Heritage Month, proclaimed by President Ronald Reagan. Black Heritage Month enjoyed significant media attention, but Hispanic Heritage Month was not given the same status. Tim Chavez dedicated a column to Hispanic Heritage Month 1997, where he wrote about David Chavez, 17 (no relation to Tim Chavez), who lived in Canandaigua, New York, about 100 miles west of Utica.[28] David had offered to write a column for the school's newspaper for Hispanic Heritage Month, as he had the previous year, but in 1997 there was no interest.

Due to many related factors, David decided to return to his native California to study at Cal State Bakersfield, located in the town to which his grandfather migrated in the early twentieth century from Mexico. He said, "I want to walk down the street and see other people who look like me."[29] David lamented the high dropout rate among Hispanics but also the fact that people falsely attributed it to poor family life. Two-thirds of Hispanic families had mothers and fathers at home. David explained that his ancestry included the Yaqui Indians in California, who were more stigmatized than his Hispanic identity. David's family did not fit many stereotypes. His brother was a journalist and his sister a teacher in an upstate school.

Jorge Hernández took over the spirit of Tim Chavez's work. Hernández had arrived in the Mohawk Valley in 1969 to study at Hamilton College. He earned his bachelor's degree at Hamilton, a master's degree at Columbia University, and a juris doctor degree from Union University/Albany Law School. He worked for 13 years as copy chief at *People* magazine. He later worked in Syracuse and, since 1995, as night local editor at the *O-D*. In 1996, he became deputy opinion page editor. He had lived in Clinton since 1997 with his wife and two children. He focused on describing personal events throughout his life which he hoped would serve as lessons to eliminate ignorance and racism. He told the story of a co-worker who had displayed a picture of his sons at his desk. Hernández told him that he would like to introduce his colleague's elder son to his daughter. His colleague responded that his mother would have a heart attack if her grandson brought home a girl named Hernández.[30] Hernández hoped that this anecdote and others would help everyone learn how otherwise intelligent people are capable of hurtful and ignorant remarks because of their lack of information about Hispanics.

Jorge Hernández, also a part-time foreign language teacher, advocated for increased language study in the area schools, offering examples from his own life as a journalist and a bilingual speaker of English and Spanish. One of his co-workers was offered a job interview by the *Wall Street Journal* because of his Spanish surname. His prospective employer was impressed with his job skills but wrongly assumed that he spoke Spanish, a skill that they expected for the position.[31] There were two important lessons in this anecdote. Not all Hispanics speak Spanish, but everyone should know a second language. A key part of language learning is its ability to remedy the false beliefs and stereotypes that give rise to racism.

Hernández focused on names, common and proper, because the way one uses them is a sign of one's understanding of various groups of people. His column in honor of Spanish Heritage Month in 1996 discussed correct generic names; it also tried to educate non-Hispanics about cultural sensitivity.[32] He, as a Puerto Rican, preferred the label *Boricua*, which refers to the natives of the island of Puerto Rico (Borinquén) before the arrival of the Spaniards. To him, the term "Hispanic" brought images of Spain's colonization and conquest of the New World, and he therefore did not wish to be associated with such a group. He did not like the term "Latino" or "Latin," which brought images of Ancient Rome and the Latin language. Since people of Spanish heritage come from so many different countries, the adjective denoting their country was preferable.

On a more personal note, his own name and the various deformations to which others had subjected it provided many examples of the need for greater understanding of the Spanish language, Hispanics, and in general, respect for people of other languages and cultures. Hernández was continually irritated by otherwise educated, well-intentioned people who would refer to him as José Rodríguez, Joyce González, George Rodríguez, George Hernández, Mr. Horseheads or even Hodge.[33] Some Uticans would tell him that he was in America now and should call himself George or "I'm going to keep calling you George until you change your name" or "In this country it's George. Don't they ever hire any local people at the newspaper?"[34] He attributed this ignorance to the lack of importance given to the study of foreign languages. Such responses evidenced the intolerance in the local area. In a light-hearted tone, he threatened to use his full name, Jorge Luis Hernández Caballero.

Hernández not only wrote about the importance of exposure to other languages and cultures, he offered opportunities to learn. During Easter week 1998, he co-chaperoned a group of twenty-three local students along with Professor Mary Stronach and others to Spain.[35] Although he was mugged in the south of Spain, he used that experience as a teaching moment for students to realize the benefits of knowing another language, along with his negotiations class from law school, in persuading the thieves to return his passport to him.

Scott Wallace was not Hispanic, and his experience with Hispanics occurred far from Utica, but his story relates to many Latinos who migrated to the U.S. in the 1990s. He was from New Hartford and grew up playing baseball and reenacting World War II battles, imitating his television heroes. Losing his desire to become a soldier after a liberal education in a New England prep school and Yale University, he ironically found himself in a war zone, specifically El Salvador in 1983, as a journalist. He was reporting one of the last Cold War confrontations, which was unfolding in Central America. As a journalist he witnessed the horrors of battles, killing and death, and how terror was used as a means of social control. People became more afraid of the threat of death than death itself. As he came into contact with the so-called communists that the U.S. government was targeting, he found that they were decent, well-educated people who were only looking for the best for their countries. They were very much like the people he grew up with in New Hartford. He could not have any influence over what was happening in Moscow or Havana, but as an American he felt an obligation to question his government. He objectively reported on what he witnessed, but he could not avoid shaping the stories to raise questions about the policies that were tearing apart families. In 1998, he returned to Utica as a reporter for the *Observer-Dispatch*. Earlier in his career he had frowned on reporting mundane local news in small circulation papers, but he wanted his three sons to experience what he had while growing up, and he realized as well that every person has a story that is worth telling.[36]

Patrick Gannon, an *Observer-Dispatch* reporter, spent a week in El Salvador in December 2001 to visit his uncle, Rev. Robert Reidy, a Roman Catholic pastor and missionary in Chiltiupán, a small mountain town in southern El Salvador.[37] El Salvador had been devastated by Hurricane Mitch in 2000 and had suffered two earthquakes in January and February 2001, which killed 1,000 people. After the earthquakes, people slowly began to rebuild. Parishioners would walk two hours just to attend Mass or sweep the church in preparation for their daughter's First Communion. Many homes, even before the earthquakes, had dirt floors and no electricity. The town's clinic had to be closed at the end of 2001 except for extreme emergency cases, because the donations from private citizens in the U.S. had stopped after the September 11 attacks. The facility had served approximately 12,000 people in an area of 90 square miles. After September 11, the impoverished villagers raised $60 to send to New York City, and many Salvadorans showed solidarity with the U.S. Over 100 Salvadorans were killed in the September 11 attacks. In recent decades the economy of El Salvador has grown increasingly dependent on the U.S., especially on the money that Salvadorans, working in the U.S., send to their relatives.[38]

CHAPTER 5

# THE SPANISH LANGUAGE: *GUAGUAS*, INTERPRETERS, AND LANGUAGE LOSS

The use of Spanish is increasing in Utica mostly because of newcomers who continue to use Spanish. Spanish can be heard in churches, restaurants, and businesses. However, its scarce presence in health care venues, social service offices, law enforcement agencies, and schools has led to issues of social injustice because of lack of adequate Spanish-speaking personnel and/or poor interpretation services. Nevertheless, the children of Spanish speakers raised in Utica inevitably grow up dominant in English because of low intergenerational transmission of Spanish in the home.[1]

As the U.S. entered the first decade of the new century, even non-Hispanics became aware of Spanglish, the title of a popular film in 2004. Latinos had been speaking Spanglish decades before the movie, even though they might not have known the term, which refers to how U.S. Latinos use both Spanish and English, often spontaneously integrating English words into Spanish. Emily Powell, born in New York City of Puerto Rican parents, but living in Utica for many years, commented on the phenomenon, "*porque con alguna familia mía yo hablo español e inglés. Empezamos en inglés y terminamos en español,* so *con todos los hispanos que yo conozco* that's how *yo hablo*" [because with some of my family, I speak Spanish and English. We start in English and finish in Spanish, so with all the Hispanics that I know, that's how I speak].[2] It is by sheer coincidence that Powell echoed the title of Shana Poplack's pioneering work on code-switching (the use of both Spanish and English in the same phrase or sentence). That article was "Sometimes I'll start a sentence in Spanish *y termino en español*" [Sometimes I'll start a sentence in Spanish and I finish in Spanish].

Román Santos, Chicano, born in California and living and working in Utica as a Spanish professor at MVCC, gave his impressions of the Spanish in Utica saying, "*Se suele oír muy poco, o por lo menos por mi experiencia, pero yo no tengo mucho contacto con la comunidad hispana aquí en Utica y los pocos con quien me comunico, la mayoría son dominicanos o puertorriqueños, entonces, se suele escuchar mucho el español del caribe o lo que un profesor mío ha llamado* United States Spanish*, o es decir, la mezcla usando la gramática del inglés pero con palabras en español.*" [You hear it very seldom or at least, in my experience, but I don't have much contact with the Hispanic community here in Utica. And the few with whom I communicate, the majority are Dominicans or Puerto Ricans, so, you hear a lot of Caribbean Spanish or what a professor of mine called United States Spanish, or that is, the mixture using English grammar but with Spanish words].[3]

Maritza Espinal of New Hartford inaugurated the *Despertar hispano-americano* column with her views relating to the transmission of the Spanish language.[4] When she arrived from the Dominican Republic in the U.S. as a little girl, she felt loneliness, not only because of the cold weather and the separation from loved ones in her homeland but also because of her weak English. Years later, after her daughter had been born, she knew that her first language would be English, but she and her husband made a conscious effort to speak to her in Spanish. They did not wish to create a linguistic barrier in their own family. At the time of the column, her daughter was growing up bilingual, speaking Spanish and learning to live in her parents' culture, while also learning English and integrating into American culture. Twenty years later, Pablo Balarezo, originally from Ecuador but living and raising his family in Utica, repeated Espinal's sentiments, "*En mi casa siempre se habla español y tratamos de que mis hijas nunca pierdan el español, y que aprendan lo más que puedan. Para nosotros es un poco de problema el inglés pero para ellas no es problema.*" [In my house Spanish is always spoken and we try so that my daughters will never lose Spanish and that they learn as much as they can. For us, English is a little bit of a problem, but for them, it isn't a problem].[5]

Jorge Novillo wrote of a newly arrived Chilean's problems adjusting not only to English, but also to the variety of Spanish spoken in Utica.[6] Sonia Basualdo had arrived in Utica in the middle of the winter of 1988, which corresponds to the middle of summer in Chile. After having walked her children to school, a teacher of Puerto Rican ancestry told her that it would be easier to return home in a *guagua* ["bus," but in Chilean Spanish, "baby"], so she asked how she could return home in a baby. The teacher stared at her in disbelief. This is just one example of the differences between Chilean Spanish and Utica Spanish, which has a heavy influence of Puerto Rican Spanish. By 1993, though, Sonia had adjusted reasonably well, and her children were doing well.

The example of *guagua* continues to be one of the clashes between Puerto Rican and South American varieties among Utican Hispanics. Marna Solete, originally from Ecuador, told of her experience with that word and with differences among the different varieties of Spanish in contact with her own, "*A veces no nos entendemos entre latinos. Los puertorriqueños dicen 'el guagua (sic).' Es el autobús. Yo les digo 'el guagua'-un bebé pequeño. Son muchas controversias porque entre latinos no nos entendemos en nuestro español.*" [At times we Latinos don't understand each other. Puerto Ricans say *'el guagua.'* It is the bus. I tell them *el guagua*—a little baby. There are many controversies because among Latinos we don't understand each other in our Spanish].[7] Pablo Balarezo gave another example of a word which his Puerto Rican sister-in-law used differently than he, "*En la comida, por ejemplo para nosotros hay una palabra que es 'sancocho' que es el cerdo ¿no?, y para ellos 'sancocho' es algo diferente.*"[8] [In food, for example, for us there is a word that is *sancocho* which is pork, no? But for them *sancocho* is something different (Sancocho is a kind of stew in Puerto Rico)].

While the different varieties of Spanish that come into contact in Utica sometimes hinder communication, at other times the Spanish language has unexpectedly united individuals. Rafael Hermoso, a new sports reporter for the *Observer-Dispatch*, was assigned to meet six new Utica Blue Sox players who had arrived for summer league play.[9] He met them at a local restaurant and introduced himself in English. Only silence followed until he asked in Spanish if any of them spoke Spanish. He saw immediate relief in their eyes, and thus a very good working relationship followed. Hermoso grew up in a Spanish-speaking household in Jamaica, Queens, NY. His father was from Spain as was his mother's family. Hermoso had never expected to use his Spanish in Utica, nor had he thought that the Latino influence in baseball would be visible in Utica.

Nicolás Ortiz, from Cidra, Puerto Rico, did not face as large a language barrier as other players because his family had moved to Chicago when he was nine years old and returned to Cidra when he was thirteen. He wanted to play baseball ever since he was a youngster.[10] His classmates, Luis Rivera and Luis López, were playing for the Boston Red Sox and San Diego Padres' Class AAA affiliate in Las Vegas. For Ortiz, baseball was more than a game—it was a way of life. Rikchy Borrero, from Mayagüez, Puerto Rico, agreed. He had been drafted as a 17-year-old to the Gulf Coast Rookie team in 1990. Borrero was forced to learn English then, actually from another Puerto Rican, Félix Maldonado, the team manager. Borrero felt comfortable speaking English but realized that many people are afraid to try, out of fear that they will be laughed at. Diogenes Baez, originally from Villa Altagracia, Dominican Republic, moved to New York City in 1981. Even though he attended Manhattan's George Washington High School, he learned little English because of the large Hispanic enrollment and classes in Spanish. He learned English at Conner State College in Oklahoma. Luis López, in his third year with the Utica Blue Sox, had limited English and always depended on someone helping him. The four players lived and spent a lot of time together. They did not feel like outsiders on the team, but they were not comfortable in the local community.

Just as the Hispanic population of Utica increased, so did the number of Spanish-speaking players who joined the Blue Sox. Latin Americans and Latinos were dominating the major league rosters. In the 1997 season, pitcher Michael Tejera had defected from Cuba, and infielders Israel Polonia,

Jorge Bautista, and Raúl Franco had arrived from the Dominican Republic.[11] Their manager, Juan Bustabad, originally from Cuba, helped them adjust to life in Utica and acted as their interpreter. Bustabad commented that there were more Spanish-speaking coaches in the minor leagues because of the greater numbers of Puerto Ricans, Dominicans, Venezuelans, and Colombians who played at that level. While there were many Latino players and coaches in Utica, Bustabad and Tejera would have liked to see more members of the local Latino community at the games. Some of the fans, though, became a social support group for the players. Sonia Martínez, originally from the Dominican Republic, but who had been in the Mohawk Valley since 1977 (when she came to attend Herkimer County Community College), and her daughter Cristina cooked meals for the players, took them grocery shopping, and drove them to the ball park. The players, who were staying in the Utica College dorms, met some students from the Dominican Republic who became their most passionate fans at the games. Rosalía Mattei, a native of Puerto Rico and a resident of North Utica, helped her friend Sonia with the meals and attended all home games, believing that it was crucial that the local community should support the players.

In his column in the *Observer-Dispatch*, Jorge Novillo wrote of the importance of learning English, but if he had not included a version in Spanish, he would not have been able to deliver his message to many area Hispanics.[12] Spanish was needed to help them transition to life in the U.S. The local cable carrier received requests to provide channels in Spanish, and "Univisión" was eventually included after a letter-writing campaign.[13] The *Observer-Dispatch* urged the new arrivals to learn English but also urged English speakers to learn Spanish.[14] Utica school teachers took courses in conversational Spanish in order to break the sense of isolation that many non-English speaking students felt. The courses were received positively and a second level was introduced. Social agencies, especially those dealing with crisis intervention, needed personnel capable of holding basic conversations with clients of limited English proficiency.

Tim Chavez grew up in Oklahoma City where there was

not a large Hispanic community. In his house, English was spoken, and although he took Spanish in high school, he never developed a high level of proficiency.[15] He was grateful for his success as a journalist, ironically due to his command of the English language, but he felt that he had lost part of his heritage because of his family's quick assimilation to life in the U.S. and shift to English. Again, ironically, if he had known Spanish, many opportunities would have opened for him, as he started his career in journalism during the time of the NAFTA treaty and the wars in Nicaragua and El Salvador. He questioned whether it was realistic to expect Hispanics to be fluent in both Spanish and English. His experience of losing the Spanish language was common among increasing numbers of Hispanics.

The Census 2000 results came out with some surprising numbers regarding language in Oneida County. The number of speakers of Spanish had risen to 5,983,[16] putting Spanish ahead of Italian. Russian and Bosnian also ranked among the top three languages other than English spoken in the area. Utica's Social Security Office had hired three bilingual Spanish/English workers and two Bosnian/English workers during the late 1990s. The Multicultural Association of Medical Interpreters of CNY (MAMI) doubled its workload from 30 to 60 hours of interpreting. About 75 percent of the requests were for Spanish, Bosnian, and Russian, particularly for older speakers of those languages. The Utica City School District had 1,200 students enrolled in the ESL program, with 29 teachers.

Tony Colón, state certified court interpreter, was a familiar face in the Oneida County Courthouse. To the relief of Zuleika Lozada, a 19-year-old Puerto Rican, he helped her fill out a form needed for her Family Court case on a February morning in 2011. She had been in Utica only ten months with her daughter and boyfriend and had limited English skills. Colón reflected on the lack of legal interpreters, saying, "There is a need for qualified legal interpreters in the community, and the unfortunate situation is there are not enough. What's happening is that there are organizations in the community that have excellent medical interpreters, but in the medical setting it is totally different."[17] Colón, owner of the Techno-Logic Solutions, was hoping to add a training course for court interpretation in his business. Legal interpreters must give a precise translation but must never provide legal advice. An interpreter who assumed an improper role could cause a disastrous outcome for the client, such as deportation or misunderstanding the consequences of a plea agreement. Court workers and police had been making more calls to MAMI, which, although focused on medical interpretation, planned to offer training for them. Cornelia Brown, Director of MAMI, explained the situation, saying, "we see a lot of different cultural barriers for people in courts. The Burmese and Somalis, for example, look away from people as a sign of respect. In this country, that can be taken for a sign of shiftiness."[18] Utica City Court Judge John Balzano noticed roughly a four-fold increase in cases needing interpretation during his 12 years as judge, to 10 to 15 people per week.

Anibelkys Bonilla Guzmán, a 24-year-old Spanish speaker who left Puerto Rico and arrived in Utica in the middle of 2007, put a face on the difficulties of not knowing English in the city. It took months to get her case resolved at the Oneida County Department of Social Services.[19] She literally had to live on bread and milk, obtained at local food banks, while her food stamp application was being reviewed. Her two children were not allowed to attend school because she could not pay for their physicals. Guzmán's experience was typical for Hispanic newcomers. Luz Encarnación, of the Syracuse Spanish Action League (La Liga), affirmed that there were not enough services available for the growing Hispanic population and that Utica needed to have more bilingual people in hospitals and schools. The Mohawk Valley Refugee Center worked collaboratively with the MVLA to offer services for non-refugee immigrants, including translation and interpretation. Adult school classes at the Refugee Center were also open to Hispanics, and Guzmán was taking an ESL class at the center. The center, which had experienced a sharp decrease in the number of refugees since the September 11 attacks, increased its outreach to the non-English speaking community in Utica.

Félix Rivera-Sanabria, who was 28 years old in 2009

and Spanish-speaking, also illustrated the need for Spanish services in Utica even into the first decade of the twenty-first century. His wife had left him and taken their five-year-old daughter.[20] She had gone to a women's shelter after repeated cases of domestic violence. The police had intervened several times. Rivera managed to climb to the roof of the 16-story Kennedy Plaza Apartment building (where he did not reside) and threatened to jump off. Investigator Dave Kaminski, Utica Police Department officer Hiram Ríos (who had training in suicide intervention), a Kennedy Plaza maintenance work, and a friend of Rivera (who served as interpreter) engaged Rivera for an hour and a half. A crowd formed below the building, which included his father and other relatives. Eventually the police were able to get Rivera's wife on the telephone. Rivera asked them to prove her identity by asking her to tell a personal story about his daughter. Rivera wanted to say goodbye to his daughter one last time. Satisfied that it was his wife, Rivera left with the officers, to the applause of the crowd below. He was escorted to Faxton-St. Luke's Healthcare for evaluation.

## Spanish in Health Care: MAMI to the Rescue

National reports have highlighted the issues that Hispanics had with their health status and the health care system. As a group, Hispanics have one of the worst health statuses in the nation.[21] As of the year 2000, two out of five did not have health insurance, one out of three had no family doctor or clinic, and one out of three lived below the federal poverty level. The incidence of diabetes type 2 was three times higher for Hispanics than for non-Hispanics. Hispanic women had the highest rate of cervical cancer. The third-leading cause of death among Hispanics was HIV/AIDS. At the same time, breast cancer rates were increasing fastest among Hispanic women.[22] Medical experts could not explain the jump. They urged early detection methods, such as breast self-exams and mammography. Organizations were creating bilingual hotlines, Spanish language brochures, and free or low-cost screenings. The National Hispanic Medical Association made several recommendations, including expanding health insurance coverage, making health care more affordable, and bilingual and bicultural staff at health care facilities. The American health care system, in general, struggled to serve people of different cultural backgrounds.

The local AIDS Education for Life Committee administered a 22-question survey to 200 minorities in Utica, Rome, and other smaller towns in Oneida County in the year 2000, at local churches, public housing projects, and the Gay Fair in June.[23] The group asked ministers to help in the administration of the survey because minorities tended to mistrust issues handled by whites. The individuals were asked what they thought was the cause of AIDS; 53.5 percent responded multiple sex partners, 41.9 percent alcohol/drug abuse, 32 percent gays/homosexuals. The results would be used to develop AIDS/HIV awareness programs. As national diversity increased, other medical issues, including end of life issues, challenged the U.S. medical establishment. Cultural, ethnic, and life experiences complicated how a system geared toward care of whites would deal with other groups. With Hispanics, not only was language a barrier but so were differences in cultural beliefs. In some Hispanic groups the open discussion of death means a loss of hope. What some people would consider denial, others considered terror management.[24] Other racial and ethnic groups had varying ways of dealing with these issues, so an understanding of the taboos and cultural practices was needed to ensure that the best care was delivered to patients.

The lack of Spanish medical interpreters had always been a concern for local Hispanics. Maria del Carmen Rodríguez, interviewed in 1993, always brought a translator with her each time that she took her daughter to a clinic.[25] She was learning English at the time but was not fluent enough to understand medical contexts. Although she was not required to pay the translator, she felt obligated to do so. At the time, most area hospitals had arrangements for interpreters, but patients were still told to bring along someone who could interpret for them. Some members of Hispanos Unidos met to address these concerns, and members of the Hispanic community volunteered to help interpret. Saint Luke's Memorial and Rome hospitals had a language bank (a list of interpreters for various languages). In the absence of a person, the Rome Hospital used a telephone language line to find an interpreter. St. Elizabeth's Hospital had a list of employees who could interpret. If no one was available, they called the Refugee Center.

As more and more refugees continued to arrive in the Mohawk Valley, the need for professional medical interpretation increased. Medical interpretation continued to be performed by bilingual family members, often children. Serious errors in interpreting had led to disastrous healthcare outcomes: unwanted teeth extractions because the patient did not understand what he was consenting to, or patients arriving a day late for surgery because of an error in interpretation. SUNY Institute of Technology sponsored a two-day freelance interpreting seminar in June 1998.[26] The class was taught by Maria Teresa Rojas of the New York Task Force on Immigrant Health. The material contained difficult scenarios which interpreters might face. Cornelia Brown, joint coordinator of the Utica based Multicultural Association of Medical Interpreters (MAMI), attended the event. She and Linda Kokoszki, a public health nurse for Oneida County, also argued for a standardized test for medical interpreters.

MAMI began in 1996 in a small office in the Refugee Center, but by 2001 they had 25 members and provided services every weekday in Bosnian, Russian, Spanish, and Vietnamese. MAMI was a non-profit organization, but interpreter's fees were $15 per hour for those who had passed the MAMI test and $10 per hour for others. Emergency room visits were $20 per hour. The 1964 Civil Acts Right required medical facilities to provide interpretation, free of charge, to their patients, as does the New York State Patients' Bill of Rights.

Antonia Sánchez (formerly Antonia Rodríguez, whose letter to the editor was described above) ministered at the Missionary Church of Christ on Elizabeth Street. She also worked as a MAMI translator[27] and interpreted for Linda Feliciano, a Puerto Rican who had moved to Utica, and Caridad Reyes, a Cuban immigrant.[28] Linda spoke of the isolation she felt during her doctor's visits without an interpreter. Sánchez explained the importance of translating word for word between doctors and patients. She had once accompanied a friend to the hospital whose father had heart problems. The man said in Spanish that he felt no pain but couldn't feel his legs. His daughter simply told the doctor that her father had no pain. Sánchez immediately spoke up to give an accurate and complete translation to the doctor, thus avoiding a disastrous treatment outcome for her friend's father.

The changing origins of refugees to the Mohawk Valley also changed the mix of languages needed for medical interpretation. By the end of the first decade of the new century, Vietnamese, Arabic, Burmese, and Karen were in very high demand. About 100 professional interpreters worked in the Utica area in 2009, many through MAMI. Yuki Rosario, a 25-year-old MVCC student from New York City, who attended a MAMI interpretation class, said, "When I'm in a doctor's office and I see someone who doesn't speak English, I try to help them in one way or another."[29] The class does not provide instruction in language learning but rather in techniques for accurate interpretation. Prerequisites are proficiency in English and the second language. Some officers on the Utica Police Department spoke Bosnian or Spanish, but the police usually relied on MAMI, the Refugee Center, and other agencies for help in language interpretation.

In addition to language problems in the health care venue, lack of minority nurses was an issue. Utica College received two federal grants in 2002, amounting to $946,853 to support minority students in the college's nursing program.[30] Of the 110 students enrolled in the nursing program, 62.7 percent were economically disadvantaged and 39 percent were minorities. The grants would be used for attracting and retaining students, tutoring and internship opportunities, and scholarships. The grants, awarded by the Bureau of Health Professions, the Health Resources and Services Administration, and the Department of Health and Human Services, were the largest ever awarded to a Utica College academic department.

The Spanish language in Utica has often meant much more than a linguistic system. Language shift in the family accompanies use of the dominant language and adaptation of a hybrid identity, as seen by Emily Powell's confession of mixing both English and Spanish. While Maritza Espinal, Pablo Balarezo, and Jorge Novillo stressed the importance of maintaining Spanish for cultural identity purposes and for communication needs for those whose English was weak, those same Latinos recognized the importance of English. In homes where Spanish was lost, the children ironically suffered disadvantages in their careers, such as Tim Chavez who missed out on reporting opportunities since he had never developed fluency in Spanish. Others remark that the Spanish in Utica is heavily influenced by Caribbean Spanish, which often creates conflict for speakers of South American dialects, as seen with the misunderstandings that the use of the word *guagua* causes. On the other hand, the language has served to create solidarity among Latinos of very different origins, for example, when Rafael Hermoso asked Latino baseball players whether they spoke Spanish. The growth in the number of Spanish speakers has led to the creation of new businesses, such as the MAMI interpreters and Tony Colón's Techno-Logic Solutions. On top of poor health status as a group, Spanish speakers have the added obstacle of language. Because of the urgent need, a solution was found for medical interpretation in the local area, but the stories of Anibelkys Bonilla Guzmán and Félix Rivera-Sanabria highlight the difficulties Spanish speakers continue to face in Utica in the very recent past.

CHAPTER 6

# THE WARRIOR SYMBOL

In an ironic coincidence of the calendar, National Hispanic Heritage month started on September 15, 1995, amid a series of events which outraged Latinos throughout the country. Proposition 187 in California denied educational and medical services to illegal immigrants, Cesar Chavez's name was removed from a street in Lansing, Michigan, because some citizens felt that it threatened city history, and a small apartment complex in Addison, Illinois, that housed legal Mexican immigrants was bulldozed supposedly to avoid urban blight.[1] In the same year, the city of Utica got involved in what was the largest affront to Hispanic civil rights, when a city official painted over a Hispanic-themed mural on a storefront.

In July 1995, Erik Ortiz (22) opened a small clothing store, Diamond Clothing Fashions, on the corner of Kossuth Avenue and Albany Street. He had arrived in Utica from Puerto Rico in 1993.[2] Over the course of two months he painted a mural on the building that consisted of a palm tree, a Puerto Rican flag in honor of his heritage, along with an Italian flag in honor of his grandfather, who was Italian. He explained, "It was an Italian neighborhood. I thought it was a nice way to bring two cultures together."[3] The building was owned by John Franco of Herkimer. Franco commented that the mural looked nice and he had heard many compliments by neighbors.[4] Nevertheless, some people had complained about the mural to Utica Common Councilman Patrick Yacco, D-7 (who was not the councilman in charge of that ward) and to the city codes department. Yacco maintained that Ventura's restaurant's "elite clientele shouldn't have to walk out and see some sort of warrior symbol up on the building.... We got to put a stop to this nonsense. What they had up there made no sense and it's not going to happen in my city. If you're going to do a legitimate business in Utica,

*Erik Ortiz next to his newly painted storefront. Photo Elizabeth A. Mundshenk,* Observer-Dispatch, *September 14, 1995.*

---

N.Y. we don't need no (*sic*) symbols of strength up on any building."[5] Yacco, however, could not find any city ordinances that the mural violated, so he asked the City Codes Department to get involved. Codes Enforcement Commissioner Michael Saafir could not find any codes violations either but claimed that he had convinced Franco to let him paint the building white. Saafir painted over the building, which angered Franco and provoked him to spray paint a message in red "painted by city of Utica codes department."

Public reaction to Yacco's declaration in the *Observer-Dispatch* was immediate.[6] Marilyn DeSuárez summarized the feelings of many in the Hispanic community: "For someone running for office to come out and say something like that is completely racist. I just don't understand how you can go and cover something up just because you're misinterpreting it or you don't understand it. There's no excuse for ignorance."[7] Yacco did not back down from his previous declarations and criticized Ortiz for declaring in English on the radio that he was American-Puerto Rican, yet when city officials approached him about the mural, he insisted on speaking Spanish.

Democratic mayoral candidate and city comptroller Edward Hanna and independent Barbara Klein soon weighed in on the controversy.[8] Hanna gave Erik Ortiz a check for $500 to paint a new mural, denying that the money was politically motivated. He declared that the painting over of the mural was one of numerous disgusting situations in Utica's codes department and was symbolic of Mayor LaPolla's 12-year term as mayor of the city. LaPolla acknowledged that bringing together members of Utica's Hispanic community with the neighbors who registered complaints would have been a better way to handle the issue. Barbara Klein visited Ortiz's store, just "to lend a helping hand" and left her campaign poster in the store window. Ortiz, overwhelmed by the attention, said that he and his friends planned to paint a new mural.

Public outrage continued. The mural helped to bring out some hidden but long-festering resentment in the Hispanic community. Tim Chavez affirmed that "the destruction of the storefront murals on a Hispanic business reeks of the stench of old hate for an emerging presence in the Mohawk Valley."[9] He considered the mural to be one of many racist incidents occurring frequently, such as New York Mills police taking in Laverne Carr for questioning just two hours after her son's death, Assemblyman David Townsend's insistence on reducing aid to the Oneida Indian Nation, or the lack of minority teachers in the Utica school district where one in three students was a child of color but only one in 20 teachers and administrators was a minority. Russ Davis believed the destruction of the mural to be something more than racism, "It is a scent of the rotten stew that rules Utica, a blend of power drunk, insolent arrogance mixed with contempt and sadly, more than a touch of racism."[10] He called for public apologies from Yacco, Saafir, and mayor Louis LaPolla and demanded Yacco's resignation and Saafir's dismissal. He urged the public to picket City Hall, write letters, vote, and "to become one of the sticks of dynamite that blows to bits the power structure in this town."[11]

The letter writing campaign, though, was already in the works before Davis' call. Local members of the Hispanic community, Juan Antonio Sánchez and Miriam Rivera, sent letters to the *Observer-Dispatch* that denounced the city's actions and Yacco's statements and called for apologies. Non-Hispanics, who believed that the incident was part of a bigger problem facing Utica, also wrote letters, critical of how the city had handled the issue.

Amid increasing public criticism, Pat Yacco gave his side of the story in the *Observer-Dispatch*.[12] Yacco had attended an East Utica Neighborhood Watch meeting where 65 citizens expressed concerns over "suspicious goings-on" at Erik Ortiz's shop and the "warrior-like, gang symbols" painted on the building. They asked him if the codes department could force Ortiz to paint them over. After researching the issue, Yacco found that there was no law preventing a property owner from decorating his building. The mural did not constitute any kind of code violation. As he inspected the property, though, he found an unsafe porch, exposed wiring and other violations. Yacco claimed that he did not order or even ask Saafir to paint over the mural. He defended some of his previous declarations, specifically Ventura's "elite clientele," referring to visitors such as Joe DiMaggio and Yogi Berra. He justified his interference in this problem, which was outside of his ward, as part of his obligation to listen to and act upon requests from citizens' groups such as Neighborhood Watch. In response to the accusations of racism, Yacco said that while he was proud of his own Italian heritage, he was equally proud of the Spanish class he helped to set up at the Entrepreneur Center. And he applauded Ortiz's efforts to start his own business from nothing.

Erik Ortiz and Marilyn DeSuárez organized the mural supporters into a group. Ortiz summarized the goal saying, "We plan to show unity among Hispanic people."[13] They planned a picketing demonstration to protest the painting over of the mural and to respond to Councilman Yacco's statements. The organizers obtained sixty signatures of East Utica residents who claimed that the mural did not offend them. Bart Scalise and Michael Hayes, members of the Elizabeth Street Neighborhood Watch, commented that 30 residents had attended the meeting that Yacco cited but that half of those had left before the mural was discussed.

Seven people picketed City Hall on Tuesday, September

19.[14] Messages on the signs accused city officials of racism and Yacco of bigotry and racism. Although few people picketed, they received the honks of support from motorists. Mayor LaPolla watched the protest from his office and commented that Saafir "did not react in a proper manner," but he would not issue an apology. Not only did Mayor LaPolla defend Saafir, but the African-American community leaders also did so, as Saafir was the first African-American city department head in Utica. Although only seven community members participated in the picket, fifty marchers of all ages and cultures participated in the seventh annual Unity March from Oneida Square to Hanna Park, sponsored by Utica College.[15] The message of the marchers focused on the recent turmoil involving racial insensitivity showed toward the Puerto Rican community. Scott Smith, Utica College Assistant Professor of Psychology, expressed confidence in the good will of the community that would help turn the tide of the recent conflicts.

Tim Chavez called for moderation and understanding. The Hispanic community was rightfully outraged by the removal of the mural. However, he believed that Hispanics should not call for the resignation of Michael Saafir, who had been pressured by Councilman Yacco to remove the mural. The resulting friction between the African-American and Hispanic communities was "craftily maneuvered ... to let Utica's two prominent minority groups slug it out and waste so much of the little political capital and resources both have."[16] If Saafir were fired, Utica would again have all white department heads.

Mayor LaPolla was forced to justify the city's actions to the community. He revealed the results of a report that he had ordered to explain what had happened.[17] On August 10, the city received a number of complaints from neighborhood residents and a business owner about "graffiti painted" at 916-918 Albany Street. On August 30, residents complained in person to Codes Inspector Phil Montana and Codes Director Mike Saafir. The two officials asked Erik Ortiz and his landlord if they would mind painting over the mural. Ortiz said that he had no money to buy paint. Saafir offered to buy the paint and do the painting. According to Saafir, all parties agreed to that proposal. Mayor LaPolla did not hear about this incident until after the covering had occurred. He believed that the Codes Director acted improperly and that "no one should be denied freedom of speech."[18] Efforts were made to appease East Utica residents' complaints, even though the best course of action would have been for the neighborhood residents and Ortiz to sit down and reach a mutually satisfactory agreement. LaPolla had planned a meeting with Marilyn DeSuárez, as representative of the local Hispanic community, and Mike Saafir to discuss the issue.

Comptroller Hanna weighed in again on the issue,[19] calling once more for the resignations of Yacco and the mayor and the dismissal of Saafir, accusing him of telling multiple versions of the story. The point of contention between Ortiz and Saafir was when the mural was painted over. Saafir claimed that he had done it at his own expense and on his lunch hour. Ortiz claimed that he started painting at 8:30 *a.m.* and stayed there the whole morning. Saafir responded by saying that he took his lunch at 8:30 that day.

After the regularly scheduled Utica City Common Council meeting on Wednesday, September 20, an impromptu meeting was held with twenty area Hispanics who asked Councilman Pat Yacco to account for actions and his words, especially his references to "you people."[20] Yacco responded and affirmed that he didn't do anything wrong and that he doesn't "talk with fancy words." Juan Sánchez, who attended the meeting and had initiated the petition asking for Yacco to apologize publicly to Ortiz, left the meeting feeling that the air had cleared even though Yacco had not clarified who had ordered the mural to be painted over.[21] Carmen Román, on the other hand, left the meeting with a lot of questions, "Yacco said he didn't do anything. We want to find out who did it and why."[22] She said the issue had become something more than a violation of Erik Ortiz's rights, a symbolic attack on all Puerto Ricans.

The "Building Bridges" movement was designed to tear down that which separated Mohawk Valley residents in terms of racial divisions and stereotypes. Meetings were held by several religious groups. With the controversy surrounding Erik Ortiz's mural, a lively participatory discussion was expected. One hundred fifty people had signed up to participate in five 90-minute meetings; however, they were mostly white. Tim Chavez lamented the fact that minorities did not vote in great numbers, did not participate in government and civic organizations, leaving the impression that they did not care.[23] Minorities had to start participating if they wanted better relations.

Codes Department Director Michael Saafir, the first black department head in city history, took the job in January 1994, charged with increasing codes enforcement and implementing the $1.4 million demolition program of arson-prone housing.[24] He had continually been scolded by Common Council members and especially by City Comptroller Edward Hanna, stemming from a pornographic computer program found on a codes department computer in April 1995, which turned out to have been installed in 1986 when the computer belonged to the City Data Processing Department.[25] Mayor LaPolla, James Blackshear, executive director of the Cosmopolitan Center, and Councilwoman Barbara Klein defended Saafir, expressing that he should have handled the mural controversy differently, but all things considered, he was doing a good job.

Regardless of the many local citizens' support for Saafir, his role in covering over the mural continued to be questioned, and he finally gave his side of the story. He had attended the August 30 Neighborhood Watch meeting during which residents complained about the mural. On September 8, he spoke with Ortiz, asking if he would paint it over. Ortiz responded affirmatively, as long as the city would provide the paint, adding that he wanted a burgundy color. A very short while later, Ortiz changed his mind. He would only allow his mural to be covered if other nearby property owners would paint over their wall paintings. Saafir then talked with the building's owner and Ortiz's landlord, John Franco. Saafir alleged that Franco had agreed that the mural could be painted over if the city provided the paint and the labor. Saafir left immediately to buy the paint. He started painting at 10 *a.m.* He reacted quickly because he was afraid that Franco would change his mind. Saafir claimed that Franco watched him paint but soon after he had finished, Franco painted in red letters, "Painted by the city of Utica Codes Department." Ortiz would not comment on Saafir's version of the story, since he and Franco had subsequently sued the city, and their attorney had advised them to make no further comments.[26]

Ortiz and Franco sued the city in federal court for violating their civil rights for $1.5 million. Saafir, LaPolla, and Yacco were all named in the suit. In June 1999, U.S. District Court Judge Norman A. Mordue in Syracuse recommended that all parties settle for $30,000. Ortiz and Franco agreed to $27,500. The Utica Board of Estimate and Apportionment approved the settlement on June 3. By the time of the settlement, LaPolla was no longer mayor, Saafir no longer Codes Department Director, and Yacco no longer councilman. Only LaPolla commented on the settlement, saying that he was sure that the counsel negotiated in the best manner possible.[27]

In an interview many years after the incident, the building's former owner, John Franco, commented that for the most part the *Observer-Dispatch* had accurately reported the events, however, several details did not agree with his recollection.[28] He had purchased the building from Mario Bevivino. It had been a drug store and had been closed for a long time. Franco opened up an antique shop there, but later rented it to Erik Ortiz who wished to open up a hip-hop clothes store. Ortiz hired a friend to paint the mural. Although it did show a palm tree and Puerto Rican and Italian flags, it also depicted a Roman soldier, in part to represent the Italian heritage of the area. Franco liked the mural and wanted it to remain on the building. He believed that the trouble started because Ruffy Ventura, owner of Ventura's Restaurant, might have complained to the Codes Department, Pat Yacco, and to Bart Scalise, of the East Utica Neighborhood Watch. Phil Montana, codes inspector, told Franco to get rid of it because the Roman soldier constituted graffiti. Franco asked him to define what he meant by graffiti. Montana was not able to do so. Bart Scalise also asked him when he would take off the graffiti. Barry Spina and Nick Laino, of the codes department, inspected every inch of his property, trying to find codes violations. Franco never gave Saafir permission to paint the building, but one morning, on arriving there, he saw him painting it and kicked the ladder out from under Saafir, who fell to the ground. Then, Franco painted in red, "painted by city of Utica codes department." Ortiz called the Latino Justice Agency in New York City, which sent lawyers to Utica to talk with Ortiz and Franco, who in the meantime had contacted Louis Brindisi to represent them. The lawyers from New York City offered their help, if needed. The law suit proceeded, but after Ed Hanna gave Ortiz the $500, he immediately left Utica with all of his inventory, without having informed Franco. Subsequently, Ortiz was imprisoned on unrelated charges. In 1999, when the case was about to be tried, Ortiz, still in prison, accepted the city's first offer at a pre-trial meeting because he needed the money. Brindisi and Franco wished to proceed but deferred to Ortiz. The amount of $25,000 was split among the three. Looking back, Franco agreed that the episode was indeed a violation of civil rights with racist overtones.

CHAPTER 7

# RACIAL AND ETHNIC CONFLICT

The Bridge Building Coalition took action against the numerous cries for Michael Saafir's dismissal by sending an open letter to Mayor Louis LaPolla and the *Observer-Dispatch* saying, "While we support the Hispanic community, affirm their pride in culture, and regret the intense pain brought upon the community by the painting over of the Puerto Rican flag, we fear that terminating Mr. Saafir would only allow him to be a scapegoat for even greater racial problems in this city."[1] Five white men assaulted two black men in Utica on Monday, October 23, 1995.[2] On Sunday evening, October 29, 1995, the Coalition sponsored a rally that brought 500 people to downtown Utica to hear speeches from clergy, politicians, the Oneida County NAACP, the Million Man March Committee and the African-American coalition. Although the rally was in response to the assault, the mural and the public opposition to Saafir had already sensitized the community to racial problems in the city.

The recent racially motivated issues prompted a survey of Oneida County convictions. The results showed that of the 236 people sent to New York prisons on assault charges in 1994, 251 were black or Hispanic and 79 were white.[3] Twenty percent of blacks got county jail time compared to 12 percent of Hispanics and 10 percent of whites. No Hispanics were convicted of assault or DWI in 1994, but 57.1 percent were convicted on drug-related charges, versus 38.5 percent of whites and 54.5 percent of blacks. Experts cautioned comparing such statistics, since many factors play into sentencing decisions. Nevertheless, Marc Mauer, head of the National Sentencing Project, stated that "Every time we build a prison, we know that half the cells will be filled by black males and 15 percent by Latinos."[4]

Latinos from across America gathered in Washington in

mid-October 1996 to protest another practice where Latinos were often targeted: immigration. Anthony Montoya, Mexican-American, member of Hispanos Unidos, and former Oneida County legislator, hoped that the march would renew political activism among Hispanics, as had the Million Man March among blacks in Washington in 1995. The march would help non-Hispanics become aware of an issue that especially affected Hispanics. Lee Robert, of Puerto Rican descent, remarked that Latinos were a large population in the Utica area, but were not always heard.[5]

In preparation for the 2000 Census, government workers reflected on the difficulty in categorizing people, especially those who might fit in more than one category. This concern also was evident in Oneida County's Hispanic population and was often overlooked in descriptions of the Hispanic community. Hispanics do not form one racial block. Of the 5,905 Hispanics in Oneida County at the end of the 1990s, 49.0 percent considered themselves white, 17.6 percent black, 0.7 percent Native American, 1.5 percent Asian or Pacific Islander, and 31.2 percent other.[6] The task force working on the labels recommended that Hispanic remain, but Latino or Spanish origin be permitted.[7]

At the same time, few minorities, if any, attended the Columbus parade in Utica in 1997. Blacks, Latinos, and Native Americans had very mixed feelings about celebrating Columbus. Tim Chavez related his understanding of Columbus Day, which was something that he, as a Mexican American, chose to celebrate.[8] He believed that there were lessons to be learned from Columbus, whose legacy is repeated today in many different ways. Society, in the name of righteousness, is capable of terrible things, just as are those who profess to be Christian. Those who point out the faults of others are often blinded by hypocrisy, insensitivity, and ignorance. Chavez believed that Columbus cannot personally be held responsible for what followed after his expeditions, but once greed set in, tragedy ensued. Instead of parades, Columbus Day should be a time of reflection and redirection. The debate about Columbus has continued throughout the years. Fearing that minority participation would be as low as that of Columbus Day, Chavez and *The Observer–Dispatch* urged minority participation in the Interfaith Bridge Builder Coalition's Culture Fest held in late October 1997.[9] The Coalition had become more low-key since its beginning in 1995. The Culture Fest was conceived as a new step in the group's evolution.[10] Yolanda King, the eldest child of Martin Luther King, talked at the Stanley Performing Arts Center, and other events were scheduled at area churches.

## PUERTO RICANS VERSUS THE BOSNIANS

Racial tensions plagued Utica, but so did ethnic tensions. Thirty Bosnian and Puerto Rican high school students were involved in a street fight, which took place on Friday, March 13, 1998 at 11 *p.m.* outside a bar, Nick's Place, in East Utica.[11] Bosnian witnesses reported that approximately 30 Puerto Ricans started the violence with sticks and bottles. Others said that Puerto Ricans threw rocks and bottles at the building's windows, which led to the fight outside. Several Bosnians were hospitalized for injuries. Four assault charges were filed, and police were investigating the case. Puerto Ricans would not initially comment. Assistant Principal John Kolczynski expressed fear that the tensions might continue at Proctor High School on the following Monday. The problem originated outside the Proctor High School, but with 200 Bosnian and 170 Hispanic students, school officials wished to mediate a solution, before tensions escalated. Preventive measures included adding a fifth uniformed police officer, separating Puerto Rican and Bosnian students, and having the two groups meet with social workers. Some Bosnian students did not return to school the following Monday, and others expressed fear of walking alone.

Jorge Hernández assisted in mediation. He was at first alarmed that the Puerto Rican students remained silent, which might convince people to ignore their side of the story.[12] A Hispanic mediator confessed to him that both Bosnian and Puerto Rican students were asked not to comment publicly on the issue during mediation, and that was why Puerto Rican students refused to speak with newspaper reporters. On Wednesday, March 18, an open meeting was held at Principal Ronald Mancuso's office. Hernández and *O-D* reporter Matt Leingang attended. No specific details about the events on the previous weekend were revealed. Three Puerto Rican students, two Bosnian students, and six adults discussed the conflict in general terms. The students did most of the speaking and pledged to communicate their differences with each other, rather than to fight. Legna Mejías (15) and one of the student speakers said, "If we have problems, we should be able to talk about them. I don't want to see Puerto Ricans getting hurt, and I don't want to see any Bosnians hurt."[13] Hernández praised the open and honest dialog but felt that the problem might be something bigger that could not be dismissed without voicing specifically what the concerns were. Upon talking with a colleague, who spoke plainly with Hernández about issues that might offend him as a Puerto Rican, he learned that several people in East Utica were very happy that the Bosnians were settling in the neighborhood and thus forcing out Puerto Ricans, because there was a widely held belief that Bosnians were "cleaner, more hardworking and utterly dependable."

The Building Bridges Coalition sponsored a day of diversity training for high school students at the end of April 1998, in response to the Bosnian-Hispanic conflict in Utica. Three members of the coalition, Professor Scott Smith, Devi Ramakrishnan, and Rev. John Holt, as well as Eleanor Picente (a social worker) led the Saturday session, which was eagerly endorsed by Proctor High School principal Ron Mancuso.[14] Fifteen students, from a variety of ethnic and racial backgrounds (15-18 years old), took part in the training and showed a high degree of willingness to work toward greater understanding among the different groups in the community. They were also concerned about the negative light that the conflicts shone on the area. Erlee Rodríguez, a Proctor student who also participated in the roundtable held at Proctor High School, commented, "We must learn not to judge people based on what they look like. We need to look inside every person."[15]

Just as Bosnians and Puerto Ricans fought on the streets of Utica in 1998, the results of a presidential commission on shifting demographics were revealed. The country was headed into a new century with greater ethnic and racial diversity than ever before. Hispanics would soon become the largest minority, while racial segregation and conflict would continue to increase.[16] By the year 2050, whites would not be the majority group but would not wish to give up their power and privilege. Competition and conflict among the various groups would increase.

The *Wall Street Journal* highlighted the conflict in a front page story.[17] The 3,000 Bosnian refugees who had settled in Utica from 1993 to 1999, along with some 2,500 Russian refugees, were helping the local economy by attracting some 923 jobs in the 1990s and contributing to 10 percent of local home sales. Louis LaPolla, head of the Utica Municipal Housing Authority, commented, "I don't want to say other ethnic groups are not of good quality. But they [the Bosnians] are a better quality of people than others."[18] Nevertheless, Utica's black community felt that the Bosnians' and Russians' white skin gave them an advantage over blacks. New job opportunities were systematically announced at the Refugee Center instead of the newspaper. Reverend Isaac Brown, pastor of the Salvation Ministries Full Gospel church, believed that "there's an acceptance for the refugees that isn't there for people of African-American descent."[19] The clash among Puerto Rican and Bosnian teens was attributed in part to the Hispanics' belief that the refugees were pushing them out of their neighborhoods. James Blackshear, director of the Cosmopolitan Community Center, commented on the perception that many minorities, especially Hispanics, held about the Bosnian refugees who got deals on housing opportunities and preference for job openings.[20] He could not find any evidence for such conflict and thought that new groups of people always brought differences and eventually the previous residents would accept the new people.

In less than two weeks after the *Wall Street Journal* article, yet another racial incident occurred.[21] Demetris Brooks, a black student at Proctor High School, reported that Azur Kadic, a Bosnian, called him the n-word in study hall, resulting in a fight. Both students were suspended. Demetris' mother, Annie Brooks, feared for her son's safety. Kadic's parents, through the aid of an interpreter, refused to comment. In spite of the incident, Hilda Santiago, a Proctor High School parent who helped mediate in the Bosnian-Puerto Rican fight, believed that the schools and communities were getting better at working together. She said, "We've come a long way. Our area is unique. We've had to accept different cultures for awhile now. First it was the Hispanics, then the Asians came, then Russians, and now Bosnians."[22] Jaclyn Valenti, a tenth grade student at Proctor, said, "There are still lots of separate neighborhoods in Utica. Some predominately white, some black, and some Puerto Rican. That means there's no interaction between the kids other than in school."[23]

In general, Hispanics in Utica believed that the future held more opportunities for them than for their parents and that racism would play less a part in their lives. One youth, Erwin Vera (19), a high school senior from nearby Camden, NY, commented that racism still existed, "People say that things have changed but you still hear racial jokes go around school and white people stare at black people and anyone with a Hispanic background. But young people know we have to get along better and everyone is trying harder. It may not happen in 10 or 20 years, but things will get better."[24]

The Bridge Builders conflict mediation of the Puerto Rican-Bosnian fight continued well after the first conflict. By the year 2000, an informal diversity group that the Bridge Builders had sponsored in 1998 continued to meet at Proctor High School.[25] It was formed by about 30 students, teachers, and guidance counselors to ensure that the group represented everyone at the school. The students organized study sessions and attended meetings with students at other schools. In the two years since the incident, the school had not had any further conflicts but wanted to be prepared in case tensions flared up again. Rev. John Holt, former pastor of the New Hartford First United Methodist Church, but since 2000 director of the Workforce Investment Board, indicated that problems often arose because of communication difficulties, especially with newer refugees. He thought that the students at Proctor were tolerant and respectful of differences. Holt continued to hold workshops with students.

In spite of the good will shown by many community

members, other incidents showed how racism was embedded in the Mohawk Valley. A young African-American news reporter at the *Observer-Dispatch* was called the n-word when arriving at a local home for an interview.[26] Hispanic reporters recalled phone calls in which callers insisted that they needed to change their names to American names because they were earning money in the U.S. Others reported hearing excuses for children who were painting racist graffiti on buildings, because the children didn't look Hispanic. Such behavior was reported in 2002.

CHAPTER 8

# IMPLACABLE GROWTH: THE 1990S TO THE PRESENT

Just as the mural controversy had repercussions in the 1995 Utica mayoral race, it also put the Hispanic community in the spotlight. From 1980 to 1990, Utica's Hispanic population almost doubled, from 1,230 to 2,332. Forty percent of Oneida County's Hispanic population lived in Utica. Other cities and towns experienced great increases as well: the City of Rome from 784 in 1980 to 1,714 in 1990, and Marcy, from 52 in 1980 to 976 in 1990. Marcy's and Rome's dramatic increases, however, were attributed to the opening of prisons in the 1980s. The high percentage of Latino youth promised even greater numbers of Latinos in future years, as ten percent of the school age population was Hispanic. In 1996, the National Coalition of Hispanic Health and Human Services Organization announced that Hispanic youth, 19 or younger, numbered 12 million, making Hispanics the number one minority among children.[1]

The survey conducted by Hispanos Unidos found that unemployment and lack of services in Spanish were major problems. Hispanic incomes in Oneida County had increased in 1990 but were significantly lower than for whites and higher than for blacks. Elizabeth Spraker, an ESL instructor at Oneida County BOCES, still experienced misunderstandings and discrimination because of her Spanish accent even though she had a graduate degree and spoke fluent English. Anthony Montoya, former Oneida County legislator, emphasized the lack of understanding among different groups and the importance of education and communication. Spraker and Montoya contributed to the *Observer-Dispatch's El despertar hispano-americano* columns and collaborated with Hispanos Unidos. Juan Sánchez, an account associate at ITT

Hartford Insurance Group, believed that city officials' refusal to apologize evidenced their tendency to ignore the local Hispanic community.[2]

Early Fall 1995 was an especially difficult time for the Utica Hispanic community, but their enhanced presence in the media helped to educate local non-Hispanics. The Hispanos Unidos annual *Noche de gala* (Gala/Dance Night) 1995 took on special significance, not only as a celebration of Hispanic Heritage Month but also as a way to inform the city as a whole about the Hispanic community.[3] Marilyn DeSuárez hoped that the non-Hispanics would learn about Latino culture and history and the African and Native American roots of the people. Entertainment included "Alex Torres y los reyes latinos" band from Amsterdam, NY, and two speakers, Albert Desmoines, a financial consultant from Amsterdam, and Gabriel Álvarez, a staff adviser at the Oneida County Correctional Facility. A special treat was the first public appearance of "Latin Heat Dance," a youth group sponsored by Hispanos Unidos.

The end of the 1990s saw a mass exodus from the Utica-Rome area, as thousands of residents in the 18 to 44 age group left the area after the closing of Griffiss Air Force Base and several factories. From July 1990 to July 1996, the number of people between 18 and 44 years of age in Oneida County fell from 104,464 to 92,136 (an 11.8 percent drop).[4] On the other hand, the number of Hispanics county-wide rose from 5,804 to 7,246 during the same period, an increase of 24.8 percent. The numbers of blacks, American Indians, and Asians also increased but at a lower rate than Hispanics. The county was aging but also becoming more diverse.

In the late 1990s, the potential power of Hispanic votes was understood. The national Hispanic market was recognized as considerable with a purchasing power of $348 billion.[5] Moreover, as a young population, Latinos offered corporate America a market that would be around for a long time. Latinos comprised 16 percent of the of the nation's 69.5 million youths under age 18.

In 1999, one year before the Census 2000 count, Utica and Oneida County officials were shocked with some preliminary projections by the U.S. Census Bureau, giving the city one of the largest population declines with respect to 1990 levels in the whole country.[6] With the closure of Griffiss Airforce Base and factories such as Chicago Pneumatic and Lockheed Martin, many people had indeed left the region. Nevertheless, city officials felt that the estimates were not accurate, and the Census Bureau itself admitted that its formula did not capture the Bosnian and Russian refugees. By the end of the 1990s, the area's local refugee situation was attracting national attention. Utica had the fourth highest per capita refugee population behind Chicago, St. Louis, and Phoenix.[7] From 1975 to 1998, 7,896 refugees had arrived. Among the refugees, the only Hispanics were 61 Cubans who arrived during the 1990s.

The U.S. Department of Housing and Urban Development released a surprising report in 1999, which listed Utica among the top four poorest cities in New York State, with 27.4 percent of the population living in poverty.[8] The report did not count the refugee population. The jobs that had been added in the past years were low paying service jobs, offering salaries that would be insufficient to feed a family of four. The poverty threshold for a family of four in 1998 was a yearly salary of $16,660. The poverty rate in Oneida and Herkimer Counties registered at 15.2 and 14.1 percent respectively, with a statewide average of 15 percent and a national average of 13 percent.[9]

In preparation for the 2000 Census, the Census Bureau announced that Hispanics and racial minorities tended to be undercounted, especially children. Reasons for undercounting included people not on address lists, distrust or fear of the government, and language.[10] Some 4 million people were missed in the 1990 Census. In order to avoid undercounting in 2000, special efforts were being undertaken.

The Utica Branch of the U.S. Census Bureau was the first in the state to open in December 1999. The branch planned to hire between 1,200 and 1,500 temporary workers, and 800 would work in Oneida County.[11] Provisions were made to hire individuals who spoke the languages of the community. Emphasis was placed on ensuring an accurate count of the city's growing groups, Hispanics, blacks, and refugees. The Bureau also organized volunteer committees to spread the word about the importance of being counted in the census. Hispanic and Vietnamese representatives, in particular, were scarce. Two weeks before the official Census 2000 was kicked off, the local office was releasing instructions, information, and where to seek help, especially for those who did not speak English. Diane Washington,[12] of the Utica census office, had guides available in 40 languages and contacts in the city's neighborhoods who could interpret for those having difficulty with the forms.

Two weeks before the close of the mail-in deadline, Oneida County Census reports were significantly lagging. Utica and Rome had census response rates of 54 and 60 percent respectively, with target rates of 69 and 74 percent.[13] In order to increase response rates, the local census department planned four road tours in Oneida County, with two in Utica, one at the City Center and another at the Asamblea de Iglesias Cristianas Church on John Street. In spite of involving religious leaders, distributing pamphlets at supermarkets, and the Census 2000 road tour, by the time the mail-in phase had ended, Utica was only up to a 57 percent participation rate and Rome to 62 percent.[14] Oneida and Herkimer Counties were 66 and 69 percent, respectively, with targets of 74 and 70 percent. Area residents came forward saying that they had never received forms. The Census bureau claimed that they do not send forms to post office boxes, but forms should have been hung from those residents' doors.

With the 2000 Census, students and prisoners would be counted where they were residing at the time of the Census.[15] Estimates gave a count of 3,900 students from other counties who attended Oneida County's five colleges and universities in 2000. It would be an easier task to count prisoners. As of March 2000, there were four state prisons in the county, with 5,923 inmates. The Oneida County jail had 417 inmates.

By the year 2000, there was general awareness that Hispanics had reshaped the population dynamics of the U.S. The 32 million Hispanics were not only in the border states with Mexico or large cities such as Miami and New York but were moving to smaller towns, more rural areas, and in general areas with little previous Hispanic contact.[16] This growth had impacted the workplace, the grocery store, the media, the voting booth, and the classroom. The growth was also recent. Nearly 13.1 million Hispanics had arrived in the U.S. between 1989 and 1997, and 25 percent after 1978. The main reason for immigration was the healthy economy of the late 90s that called for more workers.

As the Census 2000 unfolded, the Census Bureau received criticism of the term "Hispanic," which many considered a label that does not adequately capture the complex cultural and national mix of people of Spanish-speaking origin.[17] The Bureau defended the term as the most successful effort to identify the group. "Hispanic" was used first by the Census Bureau in the 1970 Census. In 1980 it was on the short form, and in 1990 and 2000 on all forms. The agency had struggled with a label since the 1930s to identify people of Spanish origin or descent that was understood and accepted by all. Previous labels had included "Spanish surname" or "Spanish." Hispanics, who can be of any race, represent an ethnic group rather than a racial group. The term was likely to remain because of a 1976 law that directed several departments to improve the data collection on people of Spanish origin or descent. "Latino" was also used on the Census 2000 forms.

In March 2001, the census results were released. One of the biggest surprises was the explosive growth in numbers of Hispanics, who formed the country's fastest growing group at 58 percent during the 1990s, for a total of 35.3 million (12.5 percent of the total population), which put the total number of Hispanics nearly at the same level as blacks.[18] Census 2000 allowed people to identify themselves with six groups, thus giving combinations such as non-Hispanic black or Hispanic black. The growth in the Latino population was explained by higher-than-expected rates of migration and an aggressive campaign to count Hispanics in the census. Of the 35.3 million Hispanics, approximately 47.9 percent classified themselves as white, 2 percent as black, 1.1 percent as American Indian, 0.3 percent as Asian, 42.2 percent as other race, and 6.3 percent as multiracial. Non-Hispanic whites still formed the largest group of Americans but made up only 69 percent of the total and had decreased since the 1990 Census.[19] The Census showed a decrease in the gap between numbers of males and females, who typically outnumber the former.[20] However, for every 100 Hispanic women, there were 105.9 Hispanic men. Migration patterns show that males tend to arrive first, find a job, and then call for the rest of the family.

Almost every county in New York State lost non-Hispanic white population, but the growth in minorities was slower in 36 out of the 62 counties where non-Hispanic white population registered greater than 90 percent.[21] Increases in Hispanic population were spectacular, not only in New York City and its suburbs but also in several upstate communities such as Monroe, Erie, and Dutchess Counties. Non-Hispanic whites were no longer the majority in Rochester, where their percentage had fallen to 44 percent. The Hispanic presence had prompted social service agencies to hire more bilingual staff and the United Way to track the needs of the group. The census also found that the minorities were segregated from whites, although some minorities moved to the suburbs.

The official Census 2000 figures held other surprises. Although predictions had correctly cited Utica as the biggest population loser among the cities in New York, its actual loss was 11.6 percent. The number of residents stayed above the 60,000 threshold at 60,651, down 7,986 from the 1990 Census.[22] Rome lost the most people in Oneida County, with a 21 percent drop from 1990 to 2000. The closing of Griffiss Air Force Base in 1995 was cited as the reason. Overall, Oneida County dropped from 250,836 in 1990 to 235,469 in 2000. Only the town of Marcy grew during the decade, at 9 percent. The loss of approximately 15,000 people ranked Oneida County as the nation's 12th largest loser of population.[23] New York State's population as a whole increased 5.5 percent because of growth in New York City.

Another surprise in the 2000 Census was the huge increase in Oneida County's Hispanic population. The number of Hispanics grew 30 percent, an increase of 1,741 people from 1990 to 2000, making Hispanics 3.2 percent of the county's population.[24] In the city of Utica, Hispanics increased by 1,178 people, a 50 percent rise compared to 1990. The number of Hispanics decreased slightly in Rome, from 1,714 in 1990 to 1,648 in 2000. It was the town of Marcy, though, that registered the highest relative count of Hispanics in the county, at 1,328 out of 9,469, or 14 percent. Marcy also had the highest relative number of blacks in the county, at 22 percent of the town's population. The prison in Marcy explained those increases.

Rev. Antonia Sánchez, who had been in Utica since 1960 and minister of the Missionary Church of Christ on Elizabeth Street for ten years, commented that the numbers were accurate. People came to Utica to get away from the city and the drug problems. Bleecker Street, as of 2001, had two Hispanic restaurants and one store. The work of Sánchez as a MAMI medical interpreter brought her into contact with many members of the community. Rev. Maritza Pérez, founder and minister of the Iglesia Maranatha of Rome, had seen more and more Hispanics in her congregation during the past few years, and believed that the official count of Hispanics in Oneida County would open a lot of eyes, especially in social services and other agencies.[25]

While the U.S. population as a whole was becoming more diverse, so was the Hispanic component. About 72 percent of the 35 million Hispanics counted in the 2000 Census came from the three largest components: Mexicans, Puerto Ricans, and Cubans.[26] In 2000, Mexican Americans numbered 21 million, with most of them in California, Texas, Illinois, and Arizona. The second largest group was Puerto Ricans, who had increased 25 percent to 3.4 million but did not include the 3.8 million Puerto Ricans living on the island. Puerto Ricans lived mainly in New York, New Jersey, and Pennsylvania. Cubans formed the third largest group at 1.2 million, an increase of 19 percent. Two thirds of Cuban Americans lived in Florida. In absolute terms, Salvadorans and Colombians were the largest Central and South American nationalities, respectively, but Hondurans and Ecuadorians were the fastest growing.

What the new Census showed, however, was that all numbers from Spanish-speaking countries increased, including the Dominican Republic, El Salvador and Colombia. Dominicans were the fastest growing group in the other Hispanic category, rising 32 percent to three quarters of a million people. Hispanics who were not part of the three traditional groups grew 97 percent to about 10 million. Hispanics identified more by nationality rather than by "Hispanic," "Spanish," or "Latino," a label which only one percent of all Hispanics chose in the census.

The local Hispanic community, traditionally composed of Puerto Ricans, reinforced that tendency. Of the 7,545 Hispanics in Oneida County, 4,900 were Puerto Rican, and in Utica, 4.5 percent of the city was Puerto Rican (as compared to 2.7 percent in 1990).[27] Although Puerto Rico was one of the smaller Spanish-speaking countries, it had the biggest effect on the local area. Rome's Hispanic community represented about 2.6 percent of the city, but a large part of that number included inmates in the city's two prisons.

Just as minorities were segregated on a national level, so were they segregated on a local level. Whites comprised 95 percent or higher, of the population in 36 out of Oneida County's 73 census tracts.[28] The city of Utica was the only area with any census tracts having 5 percent or more of minorities. Rural and suburban areas had few minorities; the only exceptions were colleges or prisons. Patterns of segregation began in the mid-twentieth century when more and more blacks moved into Utica. Sixty percent of the County's Hispanics lived in only 20 percent of the census tracts, concentrated along Bleecker Street in Utica. The Census 2000 revealed that 14.1 percent of Census tract 210 (the corner of Mohawk and Bleecker Streets) was Hispanic.[29] Moving east along Bleecker Street, tracts 208.03 and 208.02 were also greater than 10 percent Hispanic. The lowest relative percentage of Hispanics, 0.9 percent, was in tract 217.01 (in South Utica between Genesee, Prospect, and Oneida Streets). This was the tract that had the highest concentration of whites in the city, at 96.7 percent. The city of Rome had a smaller Hispanic population than Utica, 1,648 versus 3,510, yet it was more evenly distributed.

The town of Marcy registered the highest percentage of Hispanics in Oneida County because of its prison population.[30] Numbers from the New York State Department of Correctional Services indicated that 1,081 Hispanic inmates were housed in Marcy Correctional Facility and the Mid-State Correctional Facility. So, three out of four of Marcy's Hispanics were in prison. The prisons were also responsible for the growth in Marcy's overall population during the 1990s. It was also the only area that grew in Oneida County. Although the state prison population was decreasing, 540 more inmates lived in Marcy in 2000 than in 1990. Town Supervisor Brian Scala reported that Marcy had seen growth in housing and in new businesses, such as the Wal-Mart Distribution Center, but he hadn't seen any noticeable increase in diversity. The City of Rome housed 2,500 inmates in the Oneida and Mohawk Correctional Facilities, and 841 were Hispanic. Of the 35,000 residents in Rome, 1,648 were Hispanic.

The *Observer-Dispatch's* reporting on Hispanics in Marcy prompted Marline Vargas-Rivera to write a letter to the editor, wishing to clarify who were the true Hispanics in Marcy. She was Hispanic and lived in Marcy, yet she and her family did not reside in a correctional facility, and most likely none of the 1,081 Hispanic prisoners were from Marcy. The remaining 247 were the true Hispanic residents of Marcy, and though few in number, they did help in diversifying the town. She lamented the fact that minorities constituted large portions of the prison system and stressed the importance of education, hard work and perseverance for the children.[31]

Just as Vargas-Rivera put a human face on the census numbers of Marcy, an editorial in the *Observer-Dispatch* also reflected on the numbers as well as housing patterns and integration into the community.[32] The increasing numbers of racial minorities and Hispanics lived in segregated, small, inner city neighborhoods. Even as they moved up, they continued to be separated. Racial relations were still one of the largest unresolved issues that the nation would have to face, yet these patterns of separation and exclusion, remnants of past eras of blatant discrimination, would continue to strain relations. Segregation not only meant living in separate areas but also exclusion from opportunities. Few minorities held positions in elected government positions and government jobs. Employment opportunities were also fewer.

The Census 2000 and a study done by SUNY Albany showed that the diversity in Utica/Rome was less than in other urban areas but, even so, was accompanied by high levels of segregation.[33] The only majority/minority census tract without a prison was the Cornhill area in Utica. The whites living in that area dropped by 50 percent during the 1990s. Dissimilarity ratings, as calculated by the SUNY Albany study, were highest between blacks and whites. Segregation doesn't begin to manifest itself as a problem until residents begin to notice that they have less access to jobs, education, and public safety. This dissatisfaction had found a voice among minorities in Utica (the mural controversy, the Bosnian-Puerto Rican confrontation), but even by 2001, substantial change had not been made. Equal Opportunity Reports filed by the County showed that minorities made up 4.4 percent of the County's workforce in 1995 but only 4.3 percent in 2001. The overall minority population in Oneida County was 9.8 percent.

On a national level and taken in aggregate, Latinos were doing better than before. The Census 2000 numbers gave a picture of the potential power of the numbers of Latinos, and corporate America was reacting to those numbers.[34] The purchasing power of Hispanics jumped over 100 percent from 1990 to 2001, to a total of $452.4 billion. The Latino middle class grew 80 percent from 1980 to 2000 and Latinos were starting their own businesses. Pacific Bell was forced not only to diversify its employee ranks but also to set up a Spanish-speaking call center in California, hiring 150 bilingual workers. Businesses such as Chevron and Bank of America were actively seeking Latino workers.

Nationally, Latinos were taking more and more prominent roles in business, especially Hispanic women. The number of businesses owned by Latinas rose to 382,400 in 1996, an increase of 206 percent compared to 1987, which was the largest increase among all women.[35] Nevertheless, as a whole group, Hispanic per capita income and median household net worth ($8,830 and $4,656 in 1993, respectively) were below that of whites ($16,800 and $45,740). As of February 2002, Hispanic unemployment was at 8.1 percent, with white unemployment at 5 percent. Hispanics and African Americans were feeling the pain of layoffs in the Mohawk Valley. December 2001 had 600 fewer jobs than December 2000. Rev. Maritza Pérez of the Iglesia Maranatha in Rome said that at the beginning of 2001, almost her entire congregation was laid off, even her husband, an electrical engineer.[36] As of February 2002, four families and two single people who attended the Iglesia Maranatha were still among the city's unemployed.

The Census 2010 numbers confirmed the trends already seen in Census 2000. More than half of the increase in population from 2000 to 2010 could be attributed to Hispanics, whose total national count reached 50.4 million, compared to 35.3 million in Census 2000.[37] As in earlier censuses, the top three components of the Hispanic population were Mexican-American (31.7 million), Puerto Rican (4.6 million), and Cuban (1.7 million). The next two highest groups were Salvadorans (1.6 million) and Guatemalans (1 million). In relative terms, people from Spain were the Hispanic group that grew the fastest, to 635,253 people, six times higher than the 2000 count. Before the numbers were revealed, Hispanic counts were expected to be lower than predicted out of fear for low participation.[38] However, the number of Hispanics matched or exceeded predictions in 37 states. The greatest growth was seen in the South. Texas and Florida would be gaining representation in the House of Representatives because of Hispanics, potentially disturbing the balance of political power.

The increases at the national level were mirrored at the state and local levels. New York State's Latinos grew in number from 2.8 million in 2000 to 3.4 million in 2010, increasing in all but two cities (Hudson and Ogdensburg). Hispanics in the city of Oneida nearly doubled, and in Little Falls, in Herkimer County, nearly tripled. The 2010 Census showed 10,819 Hispanics in Oneida County, made up of 872 Mexican-Americans, 6,528 Puerto Ricans, 187 Cubans, and 3,222 other Hispanics or Latinos.[39] This represents growth at greater than 40 percent. Racial identification showed that 50 percent of Oneida County's Hispanics identified as white alone, 9.3 percent as black alone, 9.8 percent as two or more races, and 29 percent as "some other race alone." The city of Rome, whose overall population decreased, experienced an increase in Hispanics from 1,648 to 1,793, giving a citywide Hispanic composition of 5 percent. Countering fears that the region would continue to lose people, Oneida County's population rose by 591 people and the City of Utica grew by 1,584. This growth was in no small part due to Hispanics, who increased 86 percent from 3,510 to 6,555, making the city 10.5 percent Hispanic in 2010.[40]

CHAPTER 9

# HISPANIC REPRESENTATION IN GOVERNMENT AND SCHOOLS

The three-way race for Utica mayor between incumbent Republican Louis LaPolla, Democrat Barbara Klein, and Independent Edward Hanna resulted in a narrow victory for Hanna. Although the mural controversy was not attributed as a cause for Hanna's victory, it had focused negative attention on LaPolla's twelve year administration. In spite of racist criticism levied against his administration, LaPolla was the first mayor to hire a Hispanic police officer. He also hired the first black head of a city department and stood by that person when the public clamored for his dismissal. Nevertheless, no minority held the rank of sergeant or above in the police department, nor were any minority firefighters employed by the city.[1] By 2016, of the 123 firefighters in Utica, five were minorities (four percent).[2]

One of the long-standing desires of the Hispanic community was to be represented in public jobs. The county's Hispanic work force in the mid 1990s was 0.5 percent of the total, although 2.3 percent of the county population was Hispanic: five males (two employed in Streets and Highways Department, two in Police Protection, one in Broadacres County hospital) and four females (three in Public Welfare and one in Broadacres).[3] According to Equal Employment Opportunity reports, minorities were most underrepresented in the county's Corrections Division. Oneida County Executive Raymond Meier had charged his staff to recruit minorities. He was not pleased with the progress and attributed the poor showing to low minority turnout on civil service tests.[4] The county actively recruited minorities by sending announcements for civil service tests to over 250 local agencies and the local newspaper. County officials met with local church groups and organizations to promote county employment. By the end of the 1990s, the Oneida County Sheriff's Department was desperately seeking minority deputies.[5] Of 375 employees in the correctional facility, road patrol, and civil and law enforcement, there were nine Hispanic jail deputies and a few Hispanics in other divisions. In part, the increased emphasis on minority recruiting was due to urging by two Oneida County legislators, William Hendricks and John Smith, who had investigated the charges that an off-duty sheriff deputy fired a gun in a black Utica neighborhood in 1995.

Racial problems continued to increase at the Oneida County Sheriff's Department. James Brown, a suspended African-American corrections officer, filed a lawsuit against the Department for hostile working environment based on racial discrimination and unequal treatment.[6] He felt that the hostile working environment explained why so few minorities worked in the Sheriff's Department. Melva Sarahman, on the other hand, a 42-year-old Filipina and Hispanic, had worked in the department for 14 years as a corrections officer. She had heard racist and sexist comments from inmates and colleagues, but nothing was ever directed toward her, and she felt that the Sheriff's Department was a great place to work.[7] However, Pfendler Ruiz, Rome city's Diversity Coalition coordinator, was not surprised at the low number of minorities in the Sheriff's Department, echoing Brown's accusation of nepotism.[8]

By 2002, of the 1,837 Oneida County employees, 49 were black and 19 were Hispanic, 8 in the Sheriff's Department, 2 in Grounds, 3 in Health, 1 in the Youth Bureau and 5 in Social Services.[9] While these numbers represented a slight increase over previous statistics, only one percent of county employees were Hispanic, as compared to 3.2 percent of the county's population. The county continued to be pressured to remedy the situation, especially in the Sheriff's Department, where the department had been the defendant in racial discrimination cases brought by blacks.

Compared to the county, the city of Utica did somewhat better at diversifying its employment force, although not with respect to Hispanics. The city employed 603 people in

1995, with 24 minorities (four percent). In the same year, though, Utica was made up of 13.7 percent minorities. Two Hispanic males and one female were employed on the 180 member police force. One Hispanic male was employed in the Parks department. Marilyn DeSuárez denounced the low representation of Hispanics, "It makes you think all these meetings to build bridges is nothing but a crock, just a front."[10] Utica Police Chief Benny Rotundo commented that the Department had been working on minority recruitment for 30 years, recognizing the need to diversify the force to represent a diversified city.[11] As of 2014, there were 6 Hispanics (3.6 percent), 8 blacks (4.9 percent), 6 Bosnians (3.6 percent) among the city's 163 officers in the Utica Police Department.[12] The American Community Survey estimates for 2015 show Utica's Hispanics made up 13.6 percent of the city's population.

The Rome Police Department had an even lower representation of Hispanics than Utica. As of 2013, not one Hispanic was on Rome's Police Force of 76 full-time and 10 part-time officers.[13] The Department, though, was actively pursuing the recruitment of Spanish-speaking officers by working with Rev. Maritza Pérez of Rome's Maranatha Church to look for Hispanics wishing to take the civil service exam in 2013. In order to work more effectively with the Spanish-speaking citizens of Rome, several officers had taken a conversational course in Spanish at MVCC, and a few officers spoke college-level Spanish. However, that level of Spanish was not enough to deal with the needs. Rome's police officers worked with the State Police and the Oneida County Sheriff's Office to access interpreters and had recently hired the Multicultural Association of Medical/Legal Interpreters (MAMI) as a backup. One of the officers was currently training to become a certified interpreter.

County and City appointments also ignored Hispanics. President Bill Clinton had included two Hispanics in his first cabinet and one in his second. President George W. Bush's administration was 9.5 percent Hispanic. However, no Hispanic served as head of the state's 15 departments during Governor Pataki's term. Oneida County Executive Ralph Eannace and Mayor Ed Hanna had no Hispanic in their cabinets.[14] In 2001, the U.S. Office of Personnel Management cited the presence of Hispanics in federal positions at 6.6 percent, as compared to 11.6 percent in the private sector.[15]

In New York State, Hispanics were the group that most increased its voting rate in 1998. Hispanics 18 and older voted at a rate of 23.4 percent compared to 19.8 percent in 1994.[16] Puerto Ricans were becoming full participants in New York City, which had 24 elected Hispanic officials and two Congressional representatives. However, locally, as of the end of 2016, Utica had no minorities on the Common Council, and the highest appointed minority was African-American Cornell Maye, Public Safety Commissioner. The Oneida County Board of legislators had one African-American member.

Mario Colón, who unsuccessfully ran for the 5th Ward Councilman seat in the mid 1980s, presented himself for the same seat in 2008. In the years since he first ran, he had married and formed a family of four children. He earned a bachelor's degree in Elementary Education and a Master's in Elementary Education and Administration. He had served on many commissions and organizations including the United Way, the Oneida County Minority Employment Coalition, Cornhill People United, and as a parent advocate of the Mohawk Valley Youth Bureau. He emphasized that he was not running against anyone in the community. He was running to improve the issues that the community was facing, focusing in particular on safety, diversity, and improved city infrastructure. He valued diversity and felt that Uticans needed to talk to each other. He said, "It is important for people to know the contributions, characteristics, and potential of others, regardless of their ethnic origin."[17] He pledged to work toward a city budget that would improve roads, public parks, and sidewalks, looking for outside grants if necessary. He was also concerned about absentee landlords and the difficulties in maintaining their properties up to codes. He would also be favorable to enhancements of after-school programs for children. Colón was endorsed by the Republican Party of Utica. His campaign rival, Jerome McKinsey, was endorsed by the Democratic Party. Unfortunately, Colón was not successful in his second try for public office.

Sonia Martínez was the next Hispanic who ran for public office. In 2013 she was one of six candidates who ran for two vacant seats on the Utica City School Board of Education.[18] Born in the Dominican Republic, she moved to New York City in the early 1970s. She came to the Mohawk Valley in 1977 to attend Herkimer County Community College, where she earned an Associate's Degree in travel and tourism. She moved to Utica in the early 1990s and worked as a reimbursement tester and analyst for Excellus Blue Cross/Blue Shield, Utica. She decided to run for the position to serve the children and families of Utica. As a member of the community, mother, and grandmother, and in a leadership role in the Mohawk Valley Latino Organization (MVLA), she had first-hand knowledge of the students' needs and wished to try to satisfy them. Martínez decided to form the MVLA because there was not much in the way of information and resources to guide newly arrived Latinos to the area when she arrived. The language barrier was one of the biggest factors that prevented many from seeking assistance. Her goal for the association was to give one united voice to the Latino community.[19] One of the most pressing concerns of the school district was the decrease in state funding. She proposed stronger advocacy with local and state representatives and hoped to bring different groups together with contacts she had formed as founder and president of the MVLA. She had held many leadership roles in the community, which gave her experience to be an effective member of the School Board, such as Kernan and Donovan Elementary Schools Based Health Clinics, the Boy Scouts of America Council, Rebuild Mohawk Valley/Municipal Housing Agency, board member of the YWCA, NAACP Oneida County, and the Utica Public Library. Although Martínez was unsuccessful in the election, she garnered approximately 500 votes. That same year, she ran for a council-at-large seat for the Utica City Common Council. Although running as an independent, she, along with Ed Jackson, Robert Clemente, Jim Zecca, and Harmony Speciale formed a group "Utica United Party." Martínez was unsuccessful in this election bid but got, once again, approximately 500 votes.

Although not related to government workforce representation, undocumented Latino workers have found work in the area. Michael Dote pled guilty to harboring four undocumented Guatemalan workers at Scooby Rendering, Inc., a dog food plant.[20] The workers were found in 2013 after a report of a fire at the Oriskany Street plant in Utica. In early March 2017, undocumented Hispanic workers in Northern New York and some in the Mohawk Valley protested abuses on dairy farms.[21]

One bright spot in Hispanic representation in Oneida County was Oneida County Executive Anthony Picente's appointment of Anthony (Tony) Colón as trustee on the Mohawk Valley Community College Board in December 2008. Colón was the first Hispanic trustee of the college. Joan Andrek, MVCC spokeswoman, acknowledged Colón's appointment, saying, "We are very delighted to welcome Mr. Colón to the board of trustees. He is a trustee who represents diversity in his personal background that is very valuable to us."[22] Colón, from New York City and of Puerto Rican ancestry, had lived in Utica for 20 years and had founded the Techno-Logic Solutions Company in 1999, which was involved with interpreting and consulting services. Colón already held leadership positions in a number of organizations: the Oneida County Workforce Development, United Way of the Valley and Greater Utica, and the Boy Scouts of America. He was also co-founder of the Mohawk Valley Latino Association.

## HISPANICS IN THE SCHOOLS

The schools, however, had perhaps the greatest need for more minority teachers. In the Utica School District in 1995, out of the total teaching staff of 612, 19 were minorities (3.2 percent). Of the 8,171 students enrolled in all Utica schools, 3,095 (37.8 percent) were minorities, of which 707 (8.7 percent) were Hispanic. Elizabeth Spraker, member of Hispanos Unidos and instructor at Oneida County BOCES, commented, "Oftentimes the Hispanic students are overlooked for advanced classes. I think they would gain more confidence if there were more Hispanic role models in the district."[23]

As the 1990s progressed, the presence of minority teachers in Utica schools decreased. Of 627 teachers in 1998, only 1.5 percent were minorities. Minority students, though, grew to 40 percent of the student population. Margaret Reed-Shelton, a fifth grade teacher at Jefferson Elementary School (a theme-based school that promoted multiculturalism), recognized the problem, saying, "We need a faculty that better reflects our student population."[24] Jefferson Elementary had six non-white teachers, which was more than any other Utica elementary school, but it also had students from 18 different ethnic backgrounds. Utica School District Superintendent Daniel Lowengard wished to diversify the district's teachers. The low starting salaries ($24,000) put the district at a competitive disadvantage with other districts like Syracuse. Lowengard hoped to initiate a new program, "Growing your own," to encourage minority students from the district to go into careers in teaching and then train them in Utica schools.[25]

Nevertheless, the district's good intentions did not yield the expected results. By 2002, of the district's 700 teachers, only 30 (5 percent) were minorities. Among the 250 teacher assistants, 37 (15 precent) were minorities. Two of the district's 35 administrators were minorities. Maritza Espinal, a Spanish teacher assistant at Thomas Jefferson Elementary School, said, "When you have somebody who can pronounce your name, it makes such a difference. They think, 'I can be a teacher.'"[26] Children need to see people who look like them for role models and examples. The Community Foundation of Oneida and Herkimer Counties awarded the district a $107,000 grant to increase the number of minority teachers. The sum of $75,000 would become part of the "Growing your Own" program and would be spent over three years to allow teacher's assistants to return to college to earn certification.

As of the end of 2016, the Utica School District employed 7 (0.9 percent) Hispanics, 15 (2 percent) blacks and 4 (0.5 percent) Asians among 753 teachers.[27] Of the 228 teachers assistants, 18 (7.9 percent) were Hispanic, 39 (17.1 percent) black, and 4 (1.8 percent) Asian. One of the 32 administrators was black. None were Hispanic or Asian. Minorities, however, formed the majority among the students. Much more than half of the district's 10,000 students were minorities. The New York State Education Department's statistics of 2016 showed that the Utica School District was only 33 percent white, and that the Utica Academy of Science Charter School was 54 percent white.[28] In the Utica School District, minorities are the majority.

CHAPTER 10

# ESL AND EDUCATIONAL ACHIEVEMENT

A pressing issue facing the Utica School District was the English as a Second Language (ESL) program. This had been a concern for Spanish-speaking students since the early 1970s. As Utica became a major gateway for the arrival of refugees in the early 1990s, the number of students who needed ESL programs increased dramatically. Ten percent of Utica's student population was foreign-born in 1997, and 652 students were enrolled in ESL classes.[1] Spanish was one of the students' top first languages, but other languages included Bosnian, Russian, Vietnamese, and Arabic, for a total of 18-20 languages other than English. Columbus school's ESL teacher, Tania Kalavazoff, a daughter of Russian immigrants who had attended Seymour School in North Utica when there was no ESL program, understood the uniqueness of each child. She tried to teach not only the language but also the culture, which had caused problems for her as a young child. Many children arriving in Utica had never attended school and were illiterate in their first languages. As refugees, many did not start at the beginning of the school year, because they arrived at various times, even three weeks before the end of the semester. Some knew only basic words of English. Others knew nothing and often communicated with teachers and peers through gestures if there were no other students who spoke their language. Although the school district had many caring teachers, such as Kalavazoff, foreign-born students contributed so greatly to Proctor High School's drop out rate that in fall 1996 the school was put on probation.

ESL summer school classes were offered to children ages 6 to 13 at the Refugee Center, while their parents were also learning English.[2] An eight-year-old Nicaraguan boy, Lester Chavez, had been in Utica one month, and after one morning session had learned the alphabet, days of the week, and some colors. Thirty-five students were in the class sponsored by the Lutheran Immigration and Refugee Service. The program gave students who arrived too late to begin school a chance to catch up and begin the next school year on time.

Children were not the only ones enrolled in ESL classes. Their parents also needed English to work in the Mohawk Valley. The Adult ESL class at MVCC and the Refugee Center had 120 students in 1999. BOCES ESL teachers travelled to the Lutheran Home to give ESL lessons. Refugees and immigrants who were doctors and radiologists in their original countries found themselves at the bottom of the employment ladder in Utica, where even in those positions some basic ability in English was needed.

Columbus Elementary School had 180 (23 percent) of its 786 students enrolled in ESL classes in 1998.[3] About 90 percent of the ESL students were Bosnian or Russian refugees. The school was 15 percent Hispanic. Teachers always tried to introduce the culture of new students to their classmates when introducing them to their new classmates. In addition, the school celebrated a different country and culture every month. At Columbus, ESL students were integrated with other students. Twenty-two of the ESL students had Spanish as their first language, which was the fourth largest group after Bosnian (61 students), Belarussian (35 students), and Russian (31 students). Spanish-speaking students were from Cuba, the Dominican Republic, Ecuador, and Puerto Rico. The school also sent notices to parents in Spanish, Russian, and Bosnian. Funding the ESL program was a big challenge. It had grown from 5 to 28 teachers in 10 years. Superintendent Lowengard sought the help of Representative Sherwood Boehlert in securing a $500,000 federal grant. Only a fraction of that was approved ($51,000), through Boehlert's office. New York State Education Department officials promised to continue to help the district in finding grants.[4] A Federal Improvement of Education grant in the amount of $500,000 was awarded to the Utica School

District in 2001.[5] These funds were to be used for after-school ESL programming, pairing an ESL teacher with a content area teacher, teaching assistants, staff development, and technology upgrades for ESL programs. In the 2001 ESL summer program, there were 150 elementary and 100 high school students who participated, including third-grader Franchelis Molina in Sharon Eghigian's class at Columbus school. She eagerly shared with her classmates, helping those who knew less than she did.

Just as California was about to abandon its bilingual program, Utica's English as a second language program was growing. Superintendent Lowengard attributed the rise in student enrollment in the Utica School District for the year 2001-2002 to the ESL students. There were 225 new ESL students enrolled in kindergarten that year, bringing the total student enrollment to 8,744, up from 8,400 in 2000-2001.[6] To be clear, though, ESL is not a bilingual program, but rather a method to facilitate learning the English language and American culture and customs for students who speak a language other than English.

Spanish had always been one of the first languages of many students, and Hispanic students made up 10 percent of the Utica school district's students in the late 1990s. In the entire school district, 786 students took ESL classes. A total of $215,000 was budgeted for the program. ESL classes at Proctor High School were entirely conducted in English, but in simplified language. Two periods were devoted to grammar and reading and one period to one of the core subjects (for example, Global Studies). Other subjects were taught with ESL techniques, including American culture and customs.[7]

## Educational Achievement

Auditors from the American Association of School Administrators issued a warning about Utica schools in 1991, "Minorities, in the presence of biased laden behaviors and attitudes in the Utica City School District, suffer from alienation and racial isolation perpetuated by the system."[8] No male minorities in the district had earned New York State

Regents diplomas. The dropout rate was cause for concern: seven percent of the non-minorities compared to 33 percent of the minorities dropped out of high school.

The Utica School District came under fire in 1999 because of the low proportion of black students graduating with Regents diplomas, as compared to whites. In the 1998-1999 school year, 60 percent of Proctor Senior High School graduates were white, 30 percent black and 10 percent Asian and Hispanic.[9] Of the graduates, though, 80.7 percent of those earning Regents diplomas were white, 10.5 percent black, and 8.8 percent Asian and Hispanics. Data were not available for Hispanics alone, and conflating them with Asians most likely skewed the results. The New York State Education Department's April 1999 report stated that "whites and other minorities were about three times as likely as either blacks or Hispanics to earn Regents diplomas."[10]

A national study explored the high dropout rate for Hispanics. The traditional variables that explained why students leave school did not adequately describe the Latino community. In 1995-96, 12.4 percent of all Hispanic students left school, as compared to 6.4 percent of blacks and 4.5 percent of whites. Thirty percent of Hispanics in the 15-24 age group did not have a diploma, versus 12.1 percent of blacks and 8.6 percent of whites.[11] These figures had not changed from the 1980s to the 1990s. Hispanic students who spoke English as a first language dropped out at the same rate as Spanish-speaking students. The Hispanic dropout rate did not vary as a function of family income, even though this variable did follow white and black dropout rates. The only variable that could explain the difference was the lower unemployment rate of Hispanics as compared to blacks. It seemed that Hispanics left school in order to work. As time passed, the Hispanic dropout rate did not decrease.

In a Freedom of Information Act request, the *Observer-Dispatch* was able to obtain the results of the Utica city school district's eighth grade math test taken in 1999.[12] Although the article focused on black students, the results for Hispanic students were just as alarming. Hispanic students comprised 12.4 percent of all the students who took the test, yet only 6.2 percent of the students who passed it. David

Mathis, a school board member during the 1980s, tried to find solutions to the district's racial gaps then. He felt that the Utica schools operated on different levels according to race, and that blacks and minorities were less important than whites, but he did not assign blame entirely to the school. The community as a whole and the parents had to recognize the problem and do their part to find a solution. Superintendent Daniel Lowengard felt the lower test scores had nothing to do with race but rather with poverty.

Fourth-grade English language scores improved statewide in 2001.[13] In Utica, 66 percent of all fourth graders passed, with significant improvement at Kernan and Martin Luther Jr. Schools.[14] The 2002 Utica school report cards also showed increases in scores in reading and math. Scores of white students were significantly higher than those of minority students. The difference was explained as a language development problem, which resulted from economic disadvantage. Given the demographic mix of economically disadvantaged students at each school, results varied.[16] Only Kernan Elementary School failed to meet the standard although scores did improve.

In spite of the concerns about high school completion rates and test scores of Hispanic students, some local Hispanic students have thrived in the Utica schools and have been successful at the most competitive universities in the country. The Mohawk Valley Latino Association honored five students at the 12th Annual Gala, held in October, 2016. They were: Daileny Guerrero, a 2016 Gates Millennium Scholar, accepted to Barnard College class of 2020; Angel Guerrero, Syracuse University, class of 2018, majoring in Aerospace Engineering, founder and president of the Dominican Student Association and the Technology of Developing Academic Leaders Mentorship Program; Anny Guerrero, graduate of SUNY Albany 2015, with a B.S. in Human Biology, and employed at the Oneida County Workforce Investment Board; Daily Guerrero, graduate with honors of Harvard University class of 2014, and Columbia Law School graduate of 2017; Hilda Jordan, Harvard University 2019, double major in Philosophy and African American Studies. These five students were all cousins. Their parents had immigrated from the Dominican Republic and sent their children to Proctor High School.

Fewer than four out of ten Hispanic students in New York State completed a bachelor's degree within six years, as compared to six out of ten white students. In spite of their experience in local grade schools, Hispanics were successful at local colleges.[17] The *Hispanic Outlook* magazine selected SUNY Utica/Rome for inclusion in its Hispanic Outlook Tops listing of 700 U.S. colleges and universities that offered outstanding opportunities to Hispanic students in 1996.[18] Some 2,500 colleges and universities filled out comprehensive surveys about financial aid, scholarships, remedial and ESL programs, tutoring, mentoring, Latino studies departments, Spanish-heritage faculty and administrators. Dr. Shirley VanMarter, executive vice president for academic affairs, said that the listing was a source of pride for the school.

Utica College began a program with the Dominican Republic in 2009, which also indirectly touched the local Hispanic community. The program started with a trip to the Dominican Republic for seven Utica College undergraduate students in Health Studies, Occupational Therapy, and Nursing to study aging issues and to develop the students' cultural understanding and cultural competence.[19] Assistant Professor Darlene Heian organized the trip, with Sonia Martínez's help as interpreter. The students spent roughly two weeks touring a nursing home, a rehabilitation clinic, a trauma hospital and an orphanage. Subsequently, Utica College students interviewed members of the local Dominican community to assess their needs. Over time this program developed into collaborations between Utica College students and faculty and Dominican hospitals wishing to enhance their occupational and physical therapy capabilities.

Local colleges have reached out to Hispanics inside and outside of the U.S., in many different ways. Students of the Peace and Justice Action Group at Hamilton College held a fast for ten days in April 2000 to protest the U.S. Army School of the Americas, which trained soldiers implicated in some of Latin America's worst human rights violations.[20] Hamilton and Utica Colleges as well as other organizations in the Mohawk Valley contributed in fund-raising for the American Red Cross' $25 million drive to help victims of Hurricane Hortense in Puerto Rico in September 1996.[21] Latino players and coaching staff have also been part of the very successful soccer program at Herkimer College, which has dominated the championship of the National Junior College Athletic Association Division III.[22] Pepe Aragon, coach of the men's soccer team, is credited with 328 wins in 16 years as coach.[23]

CHAPTER 11

# RELIGION

Religion continued to be very important to local Hispanics in the 1990s. The Catholic Church is the traditional church in Spanish-speaking countries. Two Hispanic parishioners of Saint John's Roman Catholic Church, Maria Clara and Rosangie DelValle, were among the 600 member delegation sent from the Diocese of Syracuse to attend the 1993 World Youth Day in Denver, Colorado, presided over by Pope John Paul II. The two participated in the four-day event and returned with the desire to support area youth.[1] Rosangie DelValle, originally from Puerto Rico, stayed in Utica. As a Puerto Rican she was used to all of the holidays on the mainland — even the Fourth of July. In regards to that holiday, she celebrated as did other residents of the Mohawk Valley, with cookouts, fireworks, and time with her family.[2]

St. John's Church continued to serve the Hispanic community. In May 2002, there were 22 children from ages 7 to 18 who received First Communion during a Spanish Mass led by Rev. Luis Olguin.[3] In the 2000s while many churches in Utica were experiencing dwindling numbers of parishioners as the city's population declined, Saint Mary's of Mount Carmel Church, a traditionally Italian-American parish, was attracting many other ethnic groups, including Hispanics and Vietnamese, according to Rev. Joseph Salerno.[4] On Saint Stanislaus' 90th anniversary in 2001, Rev. Casimir Krzysiak reminded everyone of St. Stanislaus' diversity and that the church had celebrated Mass in Polish, Spanish, English, and Latin.[5] The Living Stations of the Cross, a Hispanic Lenten tradition which had been celebrated in English and Spanish in the mid 1980s by Historic Old Saint John's high school youth group, was revived in 2008 and 2009.[6]

Other Catholic traditions from Puerto Rico continued to be celebrated in Utica. The *posada*, which had been celebrated in Utica's Puerto Rican community since the 1960s, continued into the 1990s. Most of the city's Hispanics would set up a Nativity scene, and Christmas dinner would include *pasteles* (vegetable and meat pies), *coquito* (Puerto Rican egg nog), and rice pudding.[7] On January 6, 1996, Three King's Day (Feast of the Epiphany) was celebrated at the Resource Center for Independent Living.[8] The three kings, Gaspar, Melchior and Balthazar, left gifts for children, and the children filled their shoes with straw for the kings' camels. The festival held very dear memories for Edna Morales in her native Puerto Rico. She hoped that celebrations, such as the one held in Utica, would become cherished memories for her son Roy as he grew older. As a bigger issue, though, she hoped that her son would embrace Hispanic culture. Luz Soto of Utica thought that the celebration was a good opportunity to bring the Hispanic community together and learn about a tradition that many families had lost. Marilyn DeSuárez, one of the organizers of the event, explained how Hispanics, as they adopted America's Christmas traditions, lost a piece of their own heritage. The RCIL festival included games, a coloring contest, and breaking of the *piñata*.

Tony Colón said that although Catholicism might be the traditional background of many Latinos, the new evangelical Christian movements were very important, "*El movimiento hoy en día sobre la comunidad va a ser a través de las iglesias cristianas, no solamente la iglesia católica. Yo le digo que ahora hay un poco más movimiento o ahí se reúnen los hispanos, los latinos, este, también, por ejemplo, del momento que llegué a esta comunidad, yo y mi familia, somos cristianos, no somos católicos.*" [The movement nowadays in the community is going to be through Christian churches, not only the Catholic church. I tell you that now there is a little more movement or Hispanics, Latinos are gathering there, also, for example, from the time that I arrived in this community, I and my family, we are Christians, we aren't Catholics].[9]

New Hispanic Christian churches were indeed opening. Rubén Montalvo, born in Ponce, Puerto Rico, had arrived in Utica in 1987 from Newburgh.[10] He worked as a sales representative for Goya Foods, travelling from Albany to Utica to Syracuse, and since 1992, he represented Iberia Foods to local markets. In Newburgh, he and his family worshiped in a Hispanic Methodist Church. Since there was no such church in the Utica area, he and several others worshipped in homes. The evangelical movement had swept across Puerto Rico, and many had become Methodists. He and his wife Isabel had attended a few services at the Asbury United Methodist Church on Rutger Street and thought that it would make a nice church for Hispanic people. Five years later, Montalvo met retired clergyman Rev. Robert W. Bird and asked if his Hispanic group could use the building. Membership at Asbury Methodist had fallen to 120 members, with weekly attendance at 20 to 30. Both Montalvo and Rev. Bird agreed to share operating expenses and repairs, yet each would exist as a separate entity with separate services. Thus, the Iglesia Metodista Libre Hispana was born. Montalvo would serve as a lay pastor and the Free Methodist conference would provide a pastor for the duties for which Montalvo was not authorized. The two groups held a joint bilingual Christmas Eve service with songs alternating between Spanish and English. Montalvo's services would be exclusively in Spanish, but since the church was open to all, translations of the hymns would be available in English. Montalvo summarized how many Hispanics felt about religion when he said, "We do many things the American way. The one thing we want to do in our own way is to worship God in our natural tongue. We also want our children to learn Spanish."[11]

One of the first actions of the Iglesia Metodista Libre Hispana was to create the Coalition of Hispanic Refugees in early 1996. In August of the previous year, 45 Cuban families were resettled in the Mohawk Valley as political refugees.[12] Montalvo and his fellow parishioners wished to orient the newcomers. Many of them were skilled professionals but needed help learning the language, getting a driver's license, and help navigating the medical system. Eduardo Mendoza, one of the refugees, expressed his appreciation for the freedom of speech in Utica. Lydia Puig gave thanks for the opportunity and hoped that soon she and the newly arrived would contribute to the community. Salvadorans were also included among the refugees arriving in Utica at the end of the twentieth century. Erik Núñez had arrived from El

Salvador in 1996.[13] While looking for someone as a ping pong partner, he noticed the tennis courts at Chancellor Park, near his East Utica home. Although he had never played tennis, he quickly learned the sport and forged friendships with other tennis players such as Zeke Unobagha and Rev. Kenny Osuji, both from Nigeria. Rev. Osuji also spoke fluent Spanish.

The Salvation Army focused on the Latino community by assigning Eduardo and Felicidad Pilpe ministers to Utica in November 1997.[14] Felicidad, from Colombia, and Eduardo, from Ecuador, were learning English in Utica. Under their ministry, attention was devoted to the youth in order to fight the drug problem and breakdown of the family. They started a weekly afternoon program for approximately two dozen children from 4 to 14 years of age. The sessions included a Hispanic from the community who would serve as a positive role model for the children. They heard presentations from a school teacher, a nurse, and a journalist. Each meeting was designed around a theme, for example *amistad* (friendship), and included a religious lesson from the Bible. By 1999, the Pilpes had served about 2,500 people. Some of their church members had come to the area because they had relatives in the local prisons, and as time progressed, more of their relatives settled in the area. The Pilpes emphasized education to their congregation, especially obtaining the GED, if the church member had not graduated from high school.

The Asamblea de Iglesias Cristianas church was located in a brick Victorian church building on John Street.[15] Church services were all in Spanish and filled with music and loud displays of devotion, even though church members were modest in dress and women did not cut their hair or use makeup. The Hispanic Pentecostal church consisted of 50 Puerto Ricans and 25 Dominicans. Bilingual members and English-dominant members also felt comfortable with the services in Spanish. Jacqueline Santos, a Puerto Rican student at Proctor High School, said, "Although I speak both Spanish and English, Spanish is my first language. I am comfortable. I am able to worship God in my native language."[16] Danny Zorilla, a 25-year-old student at SUNY Institute of Technology, said, "This church is similar to my hometown church.

They guide me here, advise me. I talk to the pastor and he helps me."[17] Thirty-four-year-old Pastor Raúl Candelario and his wife, Yok Ling, were recruited by the congregation in 1996. Coming from the Dominican Republic, they had difficulty adjusting to their first winter in Utica, but they were both determined to serve the Hispanics in Utica. They believed that their message could make a positive impact on improving marriages, fighting drug addiction and delinquency, and helping everyone to become better citizens.

Wilfredo Rosario and his wife Aurea moved their family from New York City to Pennsylvania and on to Rome, NY, trying to find a place to shelter their children Mildred (22), Aurea (17), Emanuel (14), and Josue (11) from crime and drugs.[18] He and his wife struggled to put their children through school, and all children, when possible, found outside jobs to help. The children did very well in school. Mildred planned to attend medical school. She worked at United Cerebral Palsy to help earn money for college. Some people considered her a role model for young Hispanics. Aurea, soon to graduate from high school, planned to get her R.N. license. Emanuel aspired to be a lawyer. He was in honors classes and treasurer of his class. The Rosarios were active members of the Iglesia Maranatha in Rome. Wilfredo was co-pastor and his wife treasurer. Mildred was a secretary and taught Sunday school. Rev. Maritza Pérez, founder of the church, commented that non-Hispanics often saw Hispanics in a negative light. However, doctors and engineers formed part of the Rome Hispanic community. The church's members consisted primarily of Puerto Ricans, although Pérez had seen more Dominicans in the area.

Rev. Antonia Sánchez had been pastor at the Missionary Church of Christ on Elizabeth Street in Utica for ten years.[19] Her church was small, with about 27 in attendance during the week and 60 on Sunday.[20] Local Hispanics still struggled with many stereotypes but were determined to succeed. She had seen the local Hispanic population grow considerably during that time, yet more and more had arrived in recent years even though there was minimal support for them. In particular, she had seen large numbers of 20-40 year-old arrivals. She believed that many came to Utica to get away from larger cities and find a better place to live. On the other hand, Hispanics formed a diverse group of people within themselves. The community was not one cohesive unit and it needed one strong leader. Sánchez believed that more translation and interpretation services were needed. She was working with MAMI (Multicultural Association of Medical Interpreters). Sánchez had been born in Puerto Rico and moved to Utica in the 1960s. She was the Antonia Rodríguez who had written the letter to the *O-D* in 1970, in order to remind the community that many Puerto Ricans had come to Utica and relied on themselves and their families to forge a life in Utica. Her second husband Presby Sánchez passed away in 1994. She subsequently married Luis Cardona. Her memoir, *Te veo luego,* recounts the accidental death of her six-year-old daughter Peggy and how that experience tested her faith and brought her closer to God.[21] The book is a religious testimonial that takes place within the context of Utica's Puerto Rican community and is the only book to date authored by a Utican Hispanic.

In early September 2000, more than 100 Hispanic Christians marched down Bleecker Street from the corner of Bleecker and Genesee to witness publicly their culture and love for God.[22] People dressed up as Biblical characters, including children, carrying signs in Spanish and English. Rev. Martin Atayde said that the message of the day was to give an understanding of Christ, regardless of the believers' nationality. Rev. Pérez Alonso wished to highlight the Hispanic community, but God was one way to unite everyone. Antonia Sánchez urged all to plan their future, placing God first in their lives. Robert González, even though dressed as a devil, described the day as about being a Christian. Eight-year-old Marianyelis Atayde also participated in the parade, carrying a banner "God is the light of the earth."

CHAPTER 12

# THE MOSAIC OF UTICA'S LATINO COMMUNITY

## CHICANOS AND NEW MEXICANS

Mexican Americans form the largest Latino group in the country. Some Mexican Americans identify themselves as Chicanos. Although Puerto Ricans and Dominicans far outnumber Mexican Americans or Chicanos in Utica, this section gives stories of some Americans from the Southwest who have chosen to live in this community or who have had a special relationship to Utica.

Deanna Grant of Whitesboro had a unique story of finding her birth parents.[1] Deanna and her twin sister Donna White were born in Chimayo, New Mexico. Their parents, Suliema and Felipe Romero, were descendents of the Spaniards who settled in the sixteenth century in what is now the Southwestern U.S. Their ancestors had continually spoken Spanish since then. When Deanna and her sister were born, the state of New Mexico took them and three of their brothers away from their parents, who already had five children at home. All five children were put up for adoption. Mildred Boyer was working as a nurse in New Mexico when Deanna and Donna were born, and she and her husband John adopted them. After separating from her husband, Mildred returned to Whitesboro with the girls. Mildred later helped her daughters find their birthmother, who quickly answered their letters. Although the girls had thought that their mother put them up for adoption because of rejection, they found that it was poverty. Suliema and Felipe were eager to get to know their girls as well as their three sons. Deanna and Donna made a trip to New Mexico on Mother's Day in 1998. The biggest problem was the language barrier, since the Romeros spoke mostly Spanish, and Deanna and Donna, English. Deanna was surprised to find out that she was not Mexican-American, as she had originally believed, but rather, Spaniard-American. She was glad to learn more about her roots and wished she had searched sooner.

C. Fabiola Basenfelder, also originally from New Mexico, first came to the Mohawk Valley in the late 1960s to visit her sister, who had married a man from Oneida.[2] Even though she grew up in the desert, she fell in love with the Mohawk Valley. Soon after graduating from high school, she moved to the area. She felt that it was an oasis, and the greenness has appealed to her for the thirty plus years she has lived in the area. She started to work at Oneida Ltd., met her husband, and raised a family. Several of her family members followed. At first she met very few Spanish-speaking people, but by the late 1990s she witnessed the growth in the local Hispanic community.

Latin singer Jade Esteban Estrada was born at Lackland Airforce Base in San Antonio, Texas, but he felt a special bond to Utica. When he first performed in Utica in 2000, he publicly came out to the world as a gay man saying, "When I did it, I went 'Oh my God! That was me?' That was a moment where it just came out and in a moment, I made a decision that it was OK."[3] Steven Knight, PRIDE organizer, was just as surprised as everyone else when he came out in Utica. Estrada returned to Utica in 2001, as part of the Gay Pride in Central New York Celebration. He stated that he was tri-cultural: mainstream American society, Latino, and gay. In the years following his visits to Utica, Estrada became a well known, award-winning recording artist and comedian. He was invited to the White House during the Obama administration to welcome Mexican President Felipe Calderón and his wife Margarita Zavala.

Adolfo Cova, Chicano, was living and raising a family in Utica. He filled a void in the Utica radio market when he started a weekly radio program in Spanish and English (Superior 95.5) in January 2012. The program ran on Saturday afternoons until 2015, when the radio station ceased to broadcast. Cova had come to Utica from San Diego, California, several years before starting the radio program with his wife and four children. He felt welcomed in the community and started his own business, a sign business. He intended the program to be for the Latino community and said, "I think mainly this will provide Latinos the feeling they are part of the community. I hope what this boils down to is Latinos feel more integrated into the community."[4] The program featured music but also offered commentary on local news, as related to Latinos. The program was bilingual and welcomed callers from all backgrounds. Cova regularly mentioned public officials and the local Latino association MVLA, in particular Mayor Robert Palmieri and MVLA President Sonia Martínez. Although many of his criticisms seemed to be personally motivated, they help to illustrate the divisions within the local Hispanic community. He commented on Sonia Martínez's candidature for school board: "*Hay mucha gente que por allá que ha rehusado a poner esos anuncios de la Señora Sonia Martínez enfrente de su casa porque dicen 'yo aquí no quiero nada con eso.' Oye, eso me duele porque yo digo es una representación hispana pero dicen 'pero no sirve.'*" [There are a lot of people out there who have refused to put those signs of Mrs. Sonia Martínez in front of their houses because they say 'I don't want anything to do with that.' Listen, that hurts me because I say it is a Hispanic representation but they say 'but it won't work.'][5] Although Cova spoke in favor of Hispanic representation, he did not speak well of Sonia Martinez's candidacy. Instead of clearly explaining why he believed that Martínez's representation would not work, he criticized the Latino association for not advertising on his radio program.

## PUERTO RICANS

Up to the present day, the local Hispanic community consists primarily of Puerto Ricans. Several Utica Puerto Ricans and their friends will be highlighted in this section. Their stories illustrate various perspectives and experiences within the diverse group of Puerto Ricans. The section starts with the profiles of Frank Calaprice and of Vincent and Philomena Ficchi, who, although Italian-Americans, became great friends of Utica's Puerto Rican community.

Frank "Frankito" Calaprice continued to work as a secretary at the Utica Community Action headquarters in the 1980s. He had been helping Utica area Hispanics for many years, above and beyond his job description. In 1979 he founded a Spanish Religion Education Program at St. John's Church, in which 250 children were enrolled by 1985.[6] He served on the board of LAST as well as the Hispanic Action League of the 1970s, stepping in as director when no other Latino would do so. Calaprice, of Italian-American ancestry, was inspired to learn Spanish by one of his father's Spanish-speaking tenants. Subsequently he began assisting Hispanics at Historic Saint John's Church, and later professionally as director of the East Utica Community Center. He worked for 14 years at the Utica Community Action and three years as director of the Spanish Center. He represented Utica's Hispanics on 30 different boards. His most favorite activity was the Spanish First Communion program, which he founded at St John's Church. He also was instrumental in proposing an Eastern Region Spanish Apostolate in the Syracuse diocese, first headed by Rev. Amadeo Guida. As of 1985, Calaprice had changed jobs and was working as an administrative secretary for Hospice Care Inc., but he said that he would always remain involved with community work. His association with Hispanics had enriched his life with many personal friends and had showed him how a group can be American and yet still proud of its own language and heritage.[7]

Vincent and Philomena Ficchi, friends of the East Utica Puerto Rican community, became the godparents of two Puerto Rican children in 1998.[8] The Ficchis were retired and had moved out of the old neighborhood but were still invited to parties and other events of the Puerto Rican community. Vincent was the owner of V. Ficchi Heating and Air Conditioning Company on Bleecker Street, where, as of the late 1990s, he still owned 26 apartments. The Ficchis had shown many acts of kindness to the Puerto Ricans throughout the years. Vincent commented that "They've always been hard-working. And they need a helping hand. People helped the Italian immigrants when they first came. People helped my family. Now it's my turn to give something back."[9] Philomena Ficchi used to receive phone calls complaining about the doughnut wrappers that the Puerto Rican children threw on the street. Her husband always used to bring a big box of doughnuts to work and invited his tenants' children. Those doughnuts sometimes were the only breakfast that the children had. One time, Vincent paid for the ticket of one of his tenants to return to Puerto Rico to visit his mother. He had not been able to see her for a long time. When Philomena worked as a secretary at Proctor Senior High School, a young woman teacher thanked her for all she had done for her family when she was a child.

Habitat for Humanity helped Luis and Lyvel Andino, a Puerto Rican couple who arrived in the U.S. in 1995, realize their American dream.[10] Volunteers from Utica National Insurance Group and the Savings Bank of Utica donated their time and talent in fixing up 1019 Steuben Street for the Andinos and their three children. As part of the Habitat for Humanity contract, the Andinos had to spend 500 hours working on the house along with the volunteers, as well as take on a mortgage. They were able to personalize the home somewhat, with handicap accessible entrances and exits for their eldest son Roberto, who had cerebral palsy. The Andinos' home was the ninth one rehabilitated by Habitat for Humanity.

In contrast to the warm welcome that many Uticans have given Puerto Ricans, a number of Puerto Ricans have felt the sting of discrimination. Carmella Edwards, second-generation Puerto Rican, born on Long Island, moved to Utica with her family in the 1960s. She commented on her experiences during an interview in 2011 and said, "*Mis hijos no hablan español porque no querían hablar español, porque los otros estudiantes se reían de ellos. Cuando yo me mudé aquí a esta casa, ninguno de los vecinos hablaba con nosotros. No, no querían portorriqueños aquí. La discriminación es mala, pero ocurre. La gente piensan aquí en Utica que los portorriqueños están bajo, como los negros, y así ellos nos tratan todavía. Si yo voy a un restaurante o si yo voy a una tienda, a veces yo oigo la gente,* 'Oh, She's Porto Rican. She's stupid. She doesn't know anything.' *Yo no sé por qué ellos nos tratan así. Yo no sé por qué. ¿Usted sabe por qué?*" [My sons don't speak Spanish because they didn't want to speak Spanish, because the other students would laugh at them. When I moved to this house, none of the neighbors would speak to us. No, they did not want Puerto Ricans here. Discrimination is bad, but it happens. People here in Utica think that Puerto Ricans are low, as they do of the blacks, and they still treat us that way. If I go to a restaurant or if I go to a store, sometime, I hear people, "Oh, She's Porto Rican. She's stupid. She doesn't know anything." I don't know why they treat us that way. I don't know why. Do you know why?].[11]

Mario Colón noted a change in attitude of Latinos, from modest and hard-working to snobs who pretend to be what they aren't, *"La gente que estuvieron antes, ahora están en sus sesenta y cincuenta y pico y te dicen el latino aquí del cincuenta hasta el, vamos a decir, el ochenta y cuatro por ahí, fue fantástico, pero del ochenta y cuatro para acá son como nosotros llamamos 'perdonavidas.'"* [The people who were here, are now in their sixties or fifties and they tell you that the Latino here from the 1950s until, let's say, 1984 or so was fantastic, but from 1984 until now they are as we say 'braggarts'].[12] He also related what he saw as a questionable sense of Puerto Rican identity among children of Puerto Ricans born on the mainland, *"Mira, yo voy al festival de Rochester con mi esposa que viene de Ponce. Y yo le digo a ella, 'Fíjate, tanta bandera. Te apuesto cinco pesos si tú paras a ése de ahí no sabe de qué parte de Puerto Rico es.' Te entienden el español. '¿De qué parte tú eres de Puerto Rico?'* 'I ain't from Porto Rico.' 'You got the flag? What's with the flag?' 'Oh, I feel for Puerto Rico.' *¿Cómo? ¿Cómo? ¿Cómo tú vas a sentir si tus pies nunca han tocado la tierra de Puerto Rico?'"* [Look, I go to Rochester's festival with my wife who comes from Ponce. And I say to her, 'Look. So many flags. I bet you five bucks, if you stop that one over there, he won't even know what part of Puerto Rico he is from.' And they understand you in Spanish. 'What part of Puerto Rico are you from? 'I ain't from Porto Rico.' 'You got the flag? What's with the flag?' 'Oh, I feel for Puerto Rico.' How? How? How can you feel if your feet have never touched Puerto Rican soil?].[13]

On the other hand, there are children of Puerto Ricans

who do understand their Puerto Rican heritage and want to learn more Spanish, such as Erika Irizarry, born in Puerto Rico and a student at Kennedy Middle School in Utica.[14] Her parents emphasized the celebration of traditional events such as *Noche Buena* (Christmas Eve), *Día de Reyes* (Epiphany/ Three King's Day), *La abolición de la esclavitud* (abolition of slavery), *Viernes Santo* (Good Friday) and *El Día del descubrimiento de Puerto Rico* (Day of discovery of Puerto Rico, November 19). Even in Utica, her family kept alive those traditions as well as music and stories.

Ángel Jiménez, 25 in 1999 and born in Puerto Rico, moved to Utica in 1995, with the promise of a job and lower cost of living compared to New York City, where he had been raised.[15] On arriving, though, he did not have enough education or experience for many jobs in the area. He found part time work at the American Red Cross, but like many other young people, he planned to leave Utica. In any case, he would stay on the mainland because he believed that there were more opportunities for him in the U.S. than in Puerto Rico.

The first Puerto Rican restaurant was opened in Utica in 1999, Taino's Restaurant, owned and operated by Lissett Grimaldi and her parents Hector and Ether Rivera. They served Puerto Rican and traditional American food for breakfast, lunch, and dinner.[16] The restaurant could seat 40 and was located at 675 Bleecker Street. As of 2002, Taino's Restaurant was still serving the public. A second Puerto Rican restaurant, El Rincón Criollo, opened on June 10, 2000 at 672 Bleecker Street. Alma Colón, born in Ponce, Puerto Rico, had been living in Clinton for four years. Since Clinton did not have a visible Hispanic population, she thought that she would start her restaurant in Utica.[17] Menus were written in English and Spanish, and Colón felt comfortable using both languages. El Rincón Criollo was Colón's first business venture.

The Clinton School District participated in the "A Better Chance" (ABC) program where students from big city schools would attend high school in Clinton, helping to increase diversity (0.3 percent of Clinton was Hispanic according to the 2000 Census) and allowing inner-city students to experience a different kind of life. Ruben Ruiz Jr., of the Bronx, invited some of his Clinton friends to see his home during Spring Break 2002.[18] Ruiz (17) was born in Puerto Rico but raised in the South Bronx. Ruiz and fellow Puerto Rican Vladimir Rodríguez and Calvin Pamphille reflected on the stereotypes they faced when studying in Clinton. For example, people questioned whether they were in a gang or if they had ever been stabbed. In spite of the stereotypes, all three adjusted well to life in Clinton. Cindy Smiegal, Ruiz's host mother for four years, said that he had given her family much more than they could have ever given him.

*María Santa Rivera pictured here on the Rev. Franklin Upthegrove Memorial Wall, March 2017. Photo J. A. Fernández Canosa.*

Ruiz's birth mother, Caroline Ruiz, always had his favorite dish ready for him, *arroz con maíz y bistec en salsa* (rice and corn and marinated steak). She missed her son but wanted him to leave the neighborhood to get his education.

Maria Santa (Delgado) Rivera was the first Latina publicly honored in the Utica area. The Rev. Mary Webster, associate minister at St. Paul's Baptist Church, wished to honor the memory of the late Rev. Franklin Upthegrove (1921-2000), her mentor and pastor of the First Baptist Church for 28 years. Rev. Upthegrove had been a longtime community leader, working to improve race relations in Utica.[19] Interest in the project grew and the memory of twelve Uticans who had made a positive impact in the development of their neighborhoods in cultural, political, economic, religious, or educational ways were remembered on a granite memorial, the Utica Memorial Wall, at Martin Luther King Jr. Dream Park. The memorial was dedicated on May 25, 2005, and additional nominations would be sought for an annual award.

Tony Colón was part of the committee charged with

selecting a Hispanic worthy of the award. He consulted with Mario Colón who suggested María Santa after having spoken with Puerto Ricans who had arrived in Utica in the 1960s and 1970s.[20] She was well known in the community for her strong faith as a parishioner of Historic St. John's Church. María Santa was born in 1922 in Puerto Rico, where she married Hermogenes Rivera.[21] She came to Utica in 1967 and worked at Abelove Linen Co. Her husband left her and she was forced to raise her four daughters and four sons on her own. She was respected for having taken charge of a large family and *su mano fuerte* (her strong hand/a strict disciplinarian). Her children achieved successful careers, and she was considered a role model in the community. She died in 1990, leaving a family of 17 grandchildren and 3 great-grandchildren.

Although Puerto Ricans in Utica were trying to make new lives for themselves and their families, the issue of Puerto Rico's political status was of interest to many of them. Fabián Ramírez, a Puerto Rican who was visiting family in New Hartford, wrote a column in the *Despertar Hispano-americano* series, explaining three options in the 1993 plebiscite: independence, *estado jíbaro* (Puerto Rican statehood but with the condition that the island maintain the Spanish language and other traditions), and the current commonwealth (*estado libre associado*) status.[22] Since 1917 Puerto Ricans had been considered citizens of the U.S. Their status was affirmed when the island became a commonwealth in 1952. Puerto Ricans can hold U.S. passports, serve in the U.S. military, and have no travel restrictions within the U.S. They can vote for the governor of the island but cannot vote in presidential elections unless they reside on the mainland. Islanders pay no federal income taxes. They have self-government in local matters, similar to the other states. Puerto Rico has one non-voting congressional delegate. The commonwealth option prevailed in the 1993 plebiscite, but without a majority.

Given the close results of the 1993 plebiscite, Congress considered a bill in 1997 which would offer Puerto Ricans another plebiscite.[23] Utica's Puerto Ricans did not have one unified opinion on the options. Miriam Rivera wished that

Puerto Rico would maintain the current commonwealth relationship because federal taxes would cause a burden on senior citizens. Richard Cortes (26) of Utica knew people in Puerto Rico who did not back statehood because of taxes, but he felt that the result would not affect him personally. The López family who had been in Utica for five years had spent a lot of time discussing the issue of Puerto Rico's status. Nydia López, 19, interpreted for her Spanish-speaking grandmother, María López, who opted for statehood. She believed that Puerto Ricans should pay taxes and have the same rights and obligations as all other U.S. citizens.[24]

As a Puerto Rican, Jorge Hernández weighed in on the question of Puerto Rico's status and reflected on the coincidences and ironies involved in the question, which started centuries ago with a misunderstanding.[25] Supposedly, Columbus had intended to name the island San Juan, and the capital Puerto Rico (rich harbor), in honor of its commercial potential, but a cartographer mixed the two names. Ironically, the referendum that the House was considering was due for action during Hispanic Heritage Month, perhaps even near October 12, Columbus Day. The following year (1998) was the 100th anniversary of the Spanish-American War, when Spain lost all of her former colonies, Guam, Puerto Rico, the Philippines, and Cuba. Since then, Guam and Puerto Rico have been under the control of the U.S. Hernández was torn between the options of commonwealth and statehood. He himself had done very well under commonwealth status, as had many others on the island. Nevertheless, statehood would make Puerto Rico a part of the system. His 90-year-old Aunt Carmen was a staunch supporter of the U.S. and vowed to move to the mainland should the independence movement prevail. Hernández feared, though, that statehood would favor an increased pressure of American culture and business, which would erode Puerto Rican identity and uniqueness.

Because of the issue of the status of the Spanish language in the island, the legislation authorizing the plebiscite was blocked in the Senate. Governor Pedro Rosselló announced a nonbinding referendum, held in December 1998. Five options were available, and even though one option was marked "commonwealth" and another "*libre asociación*," the definition of those relationships differed from the current status. True supporters of the current relationship were urged to vote "none of the above," which won with 50 percent of the vote, versus 47 percent for statehood.[26] Puerto Rico´s status did not change. The most recently held plebiscites (in 2012 and 2017) showed a preference for statehood. Statehood legislation was introduced in the House of Representatives and Senate in 2014 but did not pass in their respective committees.

Into the 2000s, Puerto Ricans continued to form the largest component of Utica's Hispanic Community. However, second-generation Puerto Ricans were voicing their concerns about the confusion that many non-Hispanics had regarding the differences among various Latino groups. Ana Zayas-Withers, a second-generation Puerto Rican living in Utica, felt that Puerto Ricans could be a bridge for the unity of all Hispanics.[27] As U.S. citizens they could help other Hispanics become citizens or serve as interpreters. On the other hand, not all generations of Hispanic families are Spanish-speaking, and English has been the language of many families for decades. She also urged all eligible citizens to vote and at least to register if they had not yet done so.

## DOMINICANS: *VETE AL BARAJO*.

As the first decade of the twenty-first century was coming to a close, the face of East Utica was changing. Italian-American businesses that started generations ago were still thriving but were catering to new groups. Hispanics and refugees from Bosnia, Belarus, and other places were starting their own businesses. Dominicans began moving to Utica in large numbers. Some of the first Dominican businesses in Utica included Joel's Spanish-American Food at Oneida Square, the Dominican Beauty and Travel on Mohawk Street, and Family Grocery at 919 Bleecker Street, owned and run by Juan Ortiz, who had started the business in 1992. He commented that the neighborhood was deteriorating. Buildings were being demolished. People were moving away. Drugs were a major problem, so he called for greater police presence. In spite of these challenges, he had been able to stay in business.

The year 2005 was to prove conflictive for Hispanic restaurants and stores in Utica. The conflicts came from outside the Hispanic community for Nieve Núñez and from inside for Pedro Burdier. Núñez came to Utica from New York City after the September 11 attacks. She opened "Your Favorite Food Deli Grocery and Restaurant" at the corner of West and James Streets.[28] She wished to provide food for Latino customers which they could not find at other establishments. Several Uticans travelled to New York City twice per month to get those items, so her business would help avoid the long trip. The Urban Renewal Agency originally approved Núñez's business as a restaurant, not a convenience store. However, Núñez also wished to sell beer. Gene Allen, the Weed and Seed coordinator for Utica, said that many Cornhill residents felt that there were enough stores selling beer in Núñez's block. He wrote a letter to the New York State Liquor Authority to present community opposition to Núñez's application. At a Weed and Seed meeting in November 2005, no residents raised their hands in support of more alcohol sales in that neighborhood. Núñez attributed the lack of support to her being Hispanic. Councilman Bill Phillips D-5, opposed her application because the intersection at West and James Street was his worst nightmare since taking office, and beer sales would be one more reason for increased loitering at that corner, thereby aggravating neighbors' frustration even more. He denied that his opposition was at all based on Núñez's origin and said that he would be willing to sit down with Allen to discuss the issue. Núñez had been a good neighbor to nearby residents, and conditions at the intersection had improved slightly.

Milquíadez Pedro Burdier and his wife, Hilaria Soto, immigrated to the U.S. from the Dominican Republic in the early 1990s. In their first years, Burdier worked as a prep cook and Soto as a dishwasher, in Brooklyn. They had a dream to open their own restaurant. They struggled to save money, and after ten years they opened up a Hispanic restaurant in Paterson, New Jersey. After their restaurant had been opened one year, they visited friends in Utica and decided to move to the area. They bought a house and the restaurant on the corner of Bleecker and Mohawk Streets.[29] However, in the month before the restaurant's grand opening in November 2005, the name of the new restaurant caused uproar in the local Hispanic community.

Burdier wanted to name his restaurant after the restaurant in Dominican singer Zacarías Ferreira's (2005) merengue *Vete al carajo*. The song is based a play on words with the Spanish expletive *carajo* in the refrain: *Señores, estoy contento. Voy a poner un negocio. Es un restaurante que se llama 'El Carajo.' Si a alguien le molesta en la calle o el trabajo, inmediatamente, mándalo pa(ra) el carajo.* [Ladies and gentlemen. I am happy. I am going to start a business. It is a restaurant that is called 'El Carajo.' If somebody bothers you in the street or at work, send him to the Carajo]. The play on words in Spanish gives a comical sense to the phrase *mándalo para el carajo* as a way to drum up business for the new restaurant by sending annoying people to the *Carajo*. Indeed, in the least offensive sense the phrase can mean 'go away' or 'leave me alone.' However, the word *carajo* is offensive to many Spanish speakers; some would never say it. There are several obscene ways to translate the phrase into English. Nevertheless, Burdier submitted all the paperwork to the city with the name *El Carajo Restaurant*. The City of Utica did not object to the name.

In order to announce the restaurant's opening, Burdier placed several handwritten signs in the windows. Hispanic residents immediately reacted and presented complaints to Utica Codes Department. Ana Zayas-Withers, a 50-year-old second-generation Puerto Rican, commented on the restaurant's name, "It's insulting. You don't say that in a Hispanic family."[30] Utica Codes Commissioner Robert Sullivan said that the issue could raise questions about free speech, but the city would investigate the name's appropriateness, while remaining respectful of free speech rights.[31] Angelo Rodríguez, Burdier's brother, translated on behalf of his brother, who did not mean to offend anyone. The two explained that the original idea for the name came from Ferreira's merengue, and for them, the phrase simply meant 'leave me alone.' Franklin Marin (34), a Utica resident,

*El Barajo Restaurant. February 2017. Photo by J. A. Thomas.*

agreed that the phrase can mean 'leave me alone,' but it also was a swear word, "It's definitely not a positive word. Some people may think it's offensive."[32]

In an interview in September 2010, Burdier reflected on the commotion initially caused by the name, "*El pueblo en realidad de Utica no se incomodó. Los que sintieron más los, como digamos, la misma gente de nosotros, los mismos dominicanos, latinos.*" [The people of Utica really didn't get upset. The ones who felt it the most, as we say, our own people, the Dominicans themselves, Latinos.][33] He included the MVLA among those who were against the choice of the name. As the codes investigation followed, the city told Burdier that they had no problem with the name, but they did have a problem with the controversy that it had created. Burdier explained how and why he changed the name, "*Estaba hecho el letrero y estábamos discutiendo pero ya yo quería abrir el negocio. Entonces, yo, para abrir, decidí, nosotros decimos los dominicanos, 'barajar,' es como cuando usted quiere hacer una cosa y no la hizo, no la pudo hacer. Se me barajó el plan. Entonces, como había una 'c,' carajo, vamos a hacer una 'b,' que diga 'barajo.'*"[34] [So, I already had the sign made. The sign was made and we were arguing but I wanted to open the business then. So, I, in order to open, I decided, we Dominicans say *barajar*, it is like when you want to do something and you didn't do it, you could not do it. My plan got messed up. So, as there was a 'c', *carajo*, we'll make a 'b', so that it says *barajo*.] This eventually earned Burdier the nickname "Barajo."

After the events, Burdier felt that the initial controversy over the name served him well, "*A mí me convino. Todo lo que pasó, todo fue a mi favor, porque el periódico venía aquí todos los días a hacer entrevistas, la televisión también. Todo el mundo estaba enfocado en esto como era la cosa latina aquí que había hecho la primera bulla."* [It was good for me. All that happened was in my favor because the newspaper was coming here every day to interview, the television too. Everyone was obsessed with this because it was the first Latino issue that had created the first uproar.]"[35] In spite of having benefitted in one way from the criticisms, Burdier still believes that the Latinos are the ones who created the uproar and that there was a certain hypocrisy in singling him out among the extremely diverse linguistic landscape of Bleecker Street with signs in various languages, *"Todo tenía que ver unos cuantos latinos porque en realidad, el americano, no le hace algo. Igualmente que ahora mismo que tenga ese bosnio o ese chino un letrero que diga lo que diga. ¿Quién entiende lo que dice?"* [It all had to do with a few Latinos because in reality, to the American, it doesn't matter to him. The same goes right now for that Bosnian or that Chinese person who has a sign that says whatever it says. Who understands what it says?].[36] He maintained that he had no intention to offend, commenting on the nature of such language, *"No hay palabra maldicha. Es la actitud que tiene la persona cuando la dice."* [There is no such thing as a bad word. It is the attitude of the person when he says it.][37]

Six months after the restaurant had opened, business was good. Hilaria Soto said, "I think people are happy because they didn't want us to use the name."[38] In spite of the initial resentment that Burdier felt toward the MVLA, Sonia Martínez, President of the association, added, "People feel welcome when they come here, like they're in their own home."[39]

Julián Iglesias, part of the ever increasing Dominican component of Utica's Hispanics, arrived in Utica in 2005 and opened Julian's Barbershop at 659 Bleecker Street. In 2007, he sold the business. The new owners moved it one block east and changed the name to the Dominican Barbershop. Iglesias continued to work there. He chose to come to Utica on the advice of a friend who spoke of Utica's safe streets, nearby countryside, and quiet nights. Through an interpreter he said, "The community accepted me right away, and everybody started coming to the barbershop. I didn't expect business to be so good."[40] Within three months of opening, Iglesias had to hire two other barbers. As of 2008, there were five barbers at the shop. Non-Hispanic businesses on Bleecker Street, however, also had to adapt. Mark Forett, who worked at NJ Flihan and Co. dealt with customers whose first languages were Chinese, Bosnian, Indonesian, and Spanish. Garro's Pharmacy had translators available and could print prescriptions in many languages. Caffè Caruso, an Italian pastry shop founded in 1938, adapted to the new Hispanic clientele, having catered several *quinceñera* parties (a traditional celebration which marks a girl's fifteenth birthday and the recognition that she is now a woman).

Iglesias was not the only Dominican who would start a barbershop. Two new barbershops, two restaurants, a grocery and deli, and a body piercing business opened in 2008. By 2008, over 40 Hispanic-owned businesses had opened in Utica and Rome. A decade earlier there was only one grocery store and no restaurants. Frank Elias, president of the Mohawk Valley Chamber of Commerce, and Angelo Roefaro, aide to Mayor David Roefaro, welcomed the opening of "Tu cocina" at Oneida Square with a ribbon cutting ceremony in 2009. The owners of the restaurant, originally from the Dominican Republic, featured Dominican dishes as well as typical local food, such as chicken riggies. Reynilda Rodríguez, sister of co-owner Francis Rodríguez, commented, "We're giving everything we have."[41]

Sylvester "Papito" Gomez opened El Toque Final Barbershop in 2008. In the three years from 2008 to 2011 his Dominican clientele increased by 20 percent. He also offered money transferring services and bill payment at his shop. El Canelo, a Mexican Restaurant that opened in South Utica in 2010 started to host a Dominican band once every three months but then increased to once a month because of its popularity, with typically at least 100 people who would attend. The Tropical Delight Nightclub and Restaurant changed hands in 2011 to another Dominican, Freddy González, who moved from Boston to Utica. He started working as a landscaper and then plowed snow in the winter. He and his co-owner, Juan Melo, continued the tradition of Dominican food, and hosted a Dominican Republic Independence Day Celebration at the Tropical Delight in February 2011.

As the decade of the teens rolled in, Dominicans were arriving to the city in noticeable numbers and were the dominant presence in Latino businesses. Of the 40 Latino businesses in the Utica area, 30 were Dominican owned and run. They included restaurants, barbershops, beauty salons, grocery stores, day care, tax services, taxis, auto repair shops, an antique store, and a *botánica* (herbal remedy shop). Luis Inoa, born in the Dominican Republic, and owner of a thriving textile business in New York City, visited some of his wife's family in Utica in the early 2000s. In 2003, he left his business and his expensive apartment in New York. He bought a duplex in Cornhill and started a grocery store in one half and lived in the other. He was glad to leave the noise and expensive living in New York City, yet he missed the presence of other Latinos. A decade or so later he said through an interpreter, "Today it's 90 percent better. In Cornhill there were houses all around where nobody lived; now, there are Latinos all around who have bought them, and it is better and cleaner."[42] Soon, relatives of the Dominicans who had settled in Utica began to move to the area directly from the Dominican Republic, increasing Utica's Dominican population from approximately 100 in 2000 to over 1,000 by 2010.

As Dominicans continued to arrive in Utica, festivals commemorating the Day of Dominican Independence were ever more present at the end of the month of February. February 27, 1844, marks the day that the Dominican Republic became independent from Haiti. Julie Malte, born in the Dominican Republic but a resident of Utica since 2006, managed Rodríguez Multi Service on Genesee Street and did much business for Dominican Independence Day.[43] Sonia Martínez organized a series of activities to celebrate the event in 2013. The Comité de Dominicanos Unidos de Utica (Committee of United Dominicans of Utica) also organized Dominican Independence Day celebrations. Their second event was held on Sunday, February 26, 2017, at the Refugee Center.

CHAPTER 13

# A NEW ASSOCIATION

The most recent organization of the Latinos in Utica is the Mohawk Valley Latino Association (MVLA), incorporated as a nonprofit organization.[1] Sonia Martínez and Tony Colón had the idea to create the association. The first meeting was held at Denny's Restaurant in Utica in October 2003. For the first year the group of four members met in Sonia's kitchen, but in April 2004, the Mohawk Valley Refugee Center gave the group some space and an office was opened. The first general membership meeting was held in 2005 and a new Executive Board of Directors elected. The group's mission is "to serve and empower the Latino community by facilitating various services, cultural events, education, and training in life skills to take on responsibilities, make decisions, and increase awareness in their own path as members of the communities in the Mohawk Valley."[2] "Motivation, Pride, Vision, and Attitude" is the association's slogan. The first MVLA sponsors were the Mohawk Valley Refugee Center, the Radisson Hotel, and then Assemblywoman Ro-Ann Destito.

Tabaré Diaz, vice president of the MVLA, who was working in the association's office in July 2004, commented that the Hispanic community was large but not together.[3] Latinos came from very different backgrounds, but language was one element that helped to bring them together. Sonia Martínez, president of the MVLA, summarized one of the goals of the organization, to help Spanish speakers have the same level of services available to English speakers. The language barrier, however, continued to be an obstacle for many Latinos. The September 11 attacks were motivating more and more Latinos to relocate to Utica from other cities. The association hoped eventually to offer programs in drug and alcohol abuse, counseling, domestic violence, job place-

*Sonia Martínez. Courtesy of Sonia Martínez.*    *Tony Colón. Courtesy of Tony Colón.*

ment, teen counseling, after-school activities, immigration assistance, purchasing a home, and health care assistance. The immediate goal was to write a grant, trying to procure $50,000 to hire an executive director, an administrative assistant, and to start some of the programs. Martínez knew about the previous association Hispanos Unidos but had not been approached by any other Hispanic organization. It could not be determined if Hispanos Unidos was still active. The MVLA was keenly aware that Hispanics tended not to be united, but to be successful, the association somehow had to overcome the divisive forces both internal and external to the community.

In Hispanic Heritage Month 2005, Tony Colón reflected on how the Hispanic presence had increased in the area, "All the numbers you see and all the statistics don't represent the true number of Hispanics who have made Utica their home. I call it the Goya section factor."[4] When Colón moved to the area from New York City in 1996 to work at Utica National Insurance, he could not find Goya products in any local stores. They were available everywhere by 2005. Martínez said, "Just driving around Cornhill, you see the changes. I see Hispanic people in the area, repairing houses and moving into the area. As I go up and down Bleecker Street, I hear people conversing in Spanish. I hear other people talking in Spanish when I'm waiting in the line at the grocery store. In 1986, when I arrived here, that wasn't happening."[5] The Hispanic community was present, whether at Joel's restaurant on Oneida Street or at the Millenium dance club on Bleecker Street, and was growing with the addition of Hispanics of different nationalities. Yelixsa Mattehews, originally from Nicaragua, lived in Utica with her mother, who had left her when she was nine months old to emigrate to Miami. It had taken nine years for the two to be reunited. Yelixsa said, "Between the political problems in my country and not having a good job, my mother wanted something better."[6]

As of 2006, the MVLA Board of Directors consisted of Sonia Martínez (president), Tony Colón (vice president), Susan Fitzgerald Culkin (treasurer), Marline Rivera (secretary), and H. Stuart De Camp (member-at-large).[7] The MVLA's first event, a dance fundraiser held in 2004, raised $700 to help with office operation. In its first two years of existence the group introduced itself and Hispanics to the community through participation in Utica Monday Nite, the Mohawk Valley Refugee Center World Festival, and the City of Utica Independence Parade. It represented the local Hispanic community in the Mohawk Valley Pride Festival and sponsored the First Hispanic Heritage Month Celebrations in 2006. MVLA representatives also sat on the Cornhill Caring Community Committee. The MVLA had begun to fulfill its goal in serving the community with the "Give the Gift of Sight" (free eye care exams and glasses for low-income residents). It facilitated information to the community about English Language Classes at the Adult Learning Center.

The association's first newsletter came out in 2006, sponsored by a grant from the New York State Family and Children's Services, as well as several Utica businesses, both Hispanic and non-Hispanic. Audrey St. Mark and Cira Foster helped to prepare the newsletter. St. Mark, who had moved from a fifth-story walk-up in upper Manhattan to three acres, a house, garage and barn, enjoyed living in the Mohawk Valley and wished to help Spanish speakers, as she had done for 13 years as a bilingual public school teacher. Cira Foster, originally from Cuba, arrived in Utica in 2000 to attend SUNYIT. She earned a degree in Telecommunications in 2003 and had been working at the Utica Public Library as an Information Technology Specialist. New members featured in the association's first newsletter included Dr. Aymmé Belén, Elizabeth Spraker, Ruth Concepción and Representative Michael Arcuri.

By 2007, the MVLA had started sponsoring a series of activities for the community. Weekly ESL classes were held at their office at the Refugee Center. The group, having always taken an interest in youth development, started a dance group for children, "Ritmo Caribeño," and offered free kickboxing lessons, also for children.[8] Ritmo Caribeño was a huge success and continues to exist. Through the years, the group has performed at the Boilermaker Race, the annual Hispanic festivals, ethnic festivals at Utica College, and at schools and other institutions. Mario Colón, MVLA member, organized the association's Hispanic Night, as part of Utica's Monday Nite Summer Heritage Celebrations for July 2007. The association strove to offer information sessions of interest to the community. Ames Immigration held a consulting session at the office, and United Healthcare was available to discuss family health insurance plans. A general membership drive was held at the Tropical Delight restaurant. Many volunteers, both Hispanic and non-Hispanic, but all interested in the local community, joined the organization. Elle Jiménez, a member since 2005, was leading the office. She also worked as a medical interpreter at St. Elizabeth's Hospital and as a part-time computer instructor. Laura Holt, a student at Hamilton College, and Jenni McFadden, who had studied in Argentina, held student internships with the association in 2007 and assisted with the ESL classes, newsletter publication, and translations. Elena Peña, originally from the Dominican Republic, helped in numerous projects, bringing along her experience in public relations and marketing. Other new members of the association in 2007 included Maria Delgado, Grace Varona, Luis García, Flerida and Yamil Peña, Marilu López Fretts, Tracy Lee Taylor, and Fabiola Basenfelder.

The MVLA often serves as the unified voice of the Latino community. Frank Elias II (president of the Mohawk Valley Chamber of Commerce), Peter Scalise (a representative from Representative Michael Arcuri's office), Frank Vescera (Utica councilman), and Phillip Haynes, (United Way) held a meeting with the MVLA at El Barajo Restaurant in March 2008.[9] The goal of the meeting was to explain to local officials something about the business culture of Latinos and the difficulties that small Hispanic businesses faced in securing financing. Frank Elias affirmed his belief that diversity was one of Utica's strengths and that he had been trying to reach out to minorities to help them in his capacity as president of the Chamber of Commerce. Tony Colón explained how cultural factors influenced Latino business owners, for example, their tendency to stay within certain boundaries and not advertise.

The MVLA used Hispanic Heritage Month (September 15-October 15, 2008) to raise awareness of Latino culture with the people of Oneida County and the surrounding area.[10] The second annual Latino festival at Hanna Park inaugurated the month of activities. One hundred people enjoyed music, dance, and Hispanic food, as well as games and activities for children. Utica College's Latin American Student Union (LASU) participated in the event.[11] Information was distributed about health and human services, voter registration, and work force development programs. The MVLA believed that attendance at such events would increase in the near future as the Latino community continued to grow. Marabella Colón, MVLA member and organizer of the event, said, "We want to share our family values, our food, our music, dancing. You don't have to be Hispanic to do the merengue or eat rice and beans."[12] Indeed, while the association advocated on behalf of Hispanics, it sought to include all groups, as its Board of Directors was made up of all ethnic groups.

Additional events scheduled for Hispanic Heritage Month included a dance class where 60 children ages 5 to 18 participated, a Latino movie night at Utica Public Library, story telling in English and Spanish, and the Fifth Annual MVLA Gala. The gala was the most popular social event organized by the MVLA and its main fund raiser. One hundred fifty people attended the event, which drew interest from non-Hispanics. "The whole community came together to support us. This wasn't just about Hispanics. It was about all cultures and trying to bring the community together," said Tony Colón.[13] The event speaker was Minerva Padilla, marketing outreach coordinator for Excellus BlueCross/ BlueShield. As a third-generation Puerto Rican, she relied heavily on her family's experience in her daily work. Her talk focused on the struggles that the Latino community faces in society and the ways in which agencies try to help them. "There are a lot of barriers to cross with the Hispanic culture. It's not just about the language. They come to live in this country, but they never let go of their culture," said Padilla.[14] Sonia Martínez reflected on the Hispanic Heritage month and said, "This month and the events have been the best so far in five years. We've had so much more interest in the events and in the organization. We set out to educate the community about the Hispanic culture and I think we did that." Just as the month was set to close, Padilla and Martínez would travel to Rochester to participate in the Second Annual Latino Upstate Summit. Daily, the MVLA continued to act as a welcome center for newly arrived Latinos, orienting them about masses in Spanish, restaurants, schools, and services. A Spanish-language GED class was planned for Fall 2008. The association had recently translated materials into Spanish for a defensive driving workshop. The MVLA represented Hispanics at local events, such as the MVCC International Festival in Spring 2009.[15]

One of the largest events that the MVLA has organized to date is the Fifth Annual Latino Upstate Summit, held at Mohawk Valley Community College on October 21, 2011. Planning for the event started approximately one year earlier. The MVLA's partners included upstate Latino associations: Hispanics United Buffalo, the Ibero-American Action League, Inc. (Rochester), La Liga Spanish Action League (Syracuse), the Centro Cívico Hispano-Americano (Albany), and the Centro Cívico of Amsterdam, Inc. The Annual Upstate Latino Summit had been founded by Hispanics United of Buffalo Executive Director Lourdes Iglesias and had been held in Buffalo (2007), Rochester (2008), Syracuse (2009) and Albany (2010). Workshops were held on the themes of youth, health, workforce and economic development, education, immigration, community, and best practices. Motivational speaker Pegine Echevarria was featured as the keynote speaker at the summit, giving a comical but yet inspirational talk focusing on self-reliance. Representatives from the Obama and Cuomo administrations attended. Following the summit, the Sixth Annual MVLA Gala was held.

# Epilogue: Work in Progess

Earl Shorris aimed to show the diversity in the national Hispanic community in his seminal book *Latinos*.[1] Jennifer Leeman in her essay "Categorizing Latinos in the history of the U.S. Census" shows how the government, by use of the labels Hispanic and Latino, lumps together a diverse group of people that have little in common.[2] Although the Utica Hispanic community is predominantly Puerto Rican, this work has shown how throughout the years, local Hispanics have struggled with this imposed identity. Even within the Puerto Rican community, diversity of experiences was evident very early on with Antonia Rodríguez's letter to the editor in 1970. Almost serving as a precursor to the English-only movement, she scolded newer Puerto Rican arrivals for demanding services in Spanish and for not immediately learning English. Forty years later, Mario Colón, born in Puerto Rico, commented on a change that he has observed in younger Puerto Ricans. Although they outwardly demonstrate affection for Puerto Rico, they have lost the language, have never set foot on Puerto Rican soil, and lack the work ethic of their ancestors. Jorge Hernández eloquently wrote how both the terms "Hispanic" and "Latino/a" were unacceptable to him, preferring "Boricua," since he was of Puerto Rican ancestry. Marna Solete and Pablo Balarezo, originally from Ecuador, and many others, have experienced similar differences, sometimes leading to confusion, in getting used to the variety of Spanish spoken in Utica.

The difficulty in bringing the local Hispanic community together shows that the labels "Hispanic" and "Latino" do not unite that group of people. Since the early 1970s, four Hispanic associations have come into existence. All began with good intentions and essentially with the same goal, to bring the Hispanic community together. The first one, the Hispanic Action League, started off with the fanfare of Milton Valladares, but when he quickly left Utica, the association struggled to survive. Frank Calaprice, a non-Hispanic, tried to keep the organization active, believing that Hispanics needed some kind of united voice. However, there was not sufficient interest in keeping the group together. The second organization, LAST, was short-lived and occupied with internal conflicts such as the voting for a beauty contest rather than advocating for Hispanics to enhance their political and workforce representation. LAST's leader Rafael Jiménez went so far as to not even consider endorsing Mario Colón for councilman in the mid 1980s, saying that the time was not right for Hispanic representation. In the 1990s Hispanos Unidos was formed, and although that group was instrumental in putting a face on the Latino community by their articles in the *Observer-Dispatch* and radio programs, as members left the area, it too slowly disappeared. The MVLA, the current association, has survived the longest but has not been fully embraced by the community. One of its founders, Sonia Martínez, has been criticized publicly, specifically by Adolfo Cova, who not only would not endorse her for the Utica School Board but came close to slandering her on his radio program. Even so, all four organizations and their presidents were called upon by the local media and politicians to represent the Latino voice of the community.

Representation in the workplace, government, and the educational system has been an issue for Hispanics in the local area ever since the first Puerto Ricans started to arrive. The percentage of Hispanics employed by Oneida County, the city of Utica, and the Utica School District has never equaled the percentage of Hispanics in the county or the city. The lack of Hispanics in such positions has prevented Hispanics from receiving social and medical services. Although the Utica Police Department has succeeded in recruiting Hispanic officers, only 3.6 percent of the force was Hispanic by 2014. The lack of Latino teachers in Utica City Schools has been similarly problematic. Teachers in the district, minority or not, have continually stressed the importance of diversity and the positive effect that minority teachers could have on minority students by serving as role models. The district has recognized the issue and tried to establish programs to enhance recruitment of minority teachers, but none have succeeded in increasing the number of minority teachers. Michael Tirado was the first and only Hispanic to sit on a city commission. Tony Colón, trustee of Mohawk Valley Community College, is the only Hispanic in the area on such a high-level board. No Hispanic has won an elected office position. Sonia Martínez and Mario Colón ran unsuccessfully for Utica City Common Council positions, and Martínez also had an unsuccessful run for Utica City School Board member in 2013.

The absence of the Spanish language in the workplace, government, and educational system has been problematic for local Hispanics. Although Claire Mar-Molinero refers to U.S. Hispanics in general, very few do not speak some English, and "the intergeneration transmission of Spanish to second and third-generations is very low."[3] Such is the case in Utica.[4] Nevertheless, there is a relationship between not having command of the majority language and inequality in the areas of job opportunities, education, and full participation in society.[5] Even into the first decade of the twenty-first century, the Utica police force was faced with incidents in which officers needed to have command of the Spanish language, for example, the case of Félix Rivera-Sanabria, who almost jumped off the Kennedy Plaza Building in 2009. The urgent need for medical interpreters has been met with some success in the founding of MAMI Interpreters in Utica. The most striking proof of language inequality leading to discrimination was given by the class action lawsuit filed by The New York Civil Liberties Union against the Utica School District on behalf of six refugee students in 2015.[6] These students had been directed into alternative programs, which could not lead to graduation, because of their ages and low abilities in English. In a separate but related case, the Utica school district was the only district sued by the State of New York based on its exclusionary enrollment policies. The case was settled in 2016 with the district's promise to change its practices. Although the suits were not filed on behalf of Latino or Spanish-speaking students, it is very likely that they also experienced the same treatment as the refugees. States such as California, Arizona, and Massachusetts have debated the many types of bilingual programs and which type of program is best for the goals of the community,[7] but Uticans have never entered such debates; simply having an effective ESL program has been a major challenge throughout the years.

The Utica Hispanic community has also been involved in conflicts with local non-Hispanics. Milagros Rodríguez lost her interpreting job in the early 1980s because of federal cuts during the Reagan administration, but neither the city of Utica nor any other public agency was able to restore her job in spite of the valuable service she provided to Hispanics. Even though Utica Hispanics have been characterized by internal strife and inability to work together, the petition drive and protests organized with the intention to restore Rodríguez's position was the first time that Hispanics came together to advocate for their mutual benefit. Rodríguez's position was not restored, but Hispanics had at last a way to reach City Hall. Urban Latino mural art has served to create ethnic pride, revitalize neighborhoods, and indeed, protest for social justice.[8] Erik Ortiz painted his storefront mural with the first two goals in mind, but after the city of Utica had painted over his storefront in 1995, the mural also became a symbol of protest for social justice. The court case was settled before trial but most likely would have been argued as a violation of Ortiz's civil rights. The city's Hispanics along with Hispanos Unidos came together and showed that they existed, were part of the community, and demanded to be treated equally. The clash between Puerto Rican and Bosnian students in 1998 in East Utica showed ethnic tension as well. The circumstances behind the fight were never revealed, although several community leaders advanced the perception that Bosnian refugees were given special treatment in job and housing opportunities and were settling into areas of East Utica that had been home to Puerto Ricans. The conflict was highlighted at a national level in the *Wall Street Journal*. The subsequent dialogue fostered among high school students by the Bridge Builders Coalition was one positive outcome of the conflict.

However, conflicts internal to the community are perhaps the ones showing the biggest obstacles to unity. Early on, Antonia Rodríguez's letter to the editor set a tone of older Puerto Rican immigrant groups versus newer groups. Mario Colón echoed a similar generational divide among Puerto Ricans 40 years earlier. In the late 1970s, it took a non-Hispanic, Frank Calaprice, to try to gather together the pieces of the Hispanic Action League that had ceased to function after Milton Valladares' quick departure. In spite of Calaprice's and others' efforts, membership dwindled and people stopped attending the meetings. The two subsequent associations met similar fates, although both did act as Hispanic community representatives. Hispanos Unidos took an active role in using the media to advocate for Hispanics and the Spanish language. Local Hispanics, specifically Pedro Burdier of the Barajo Restaurant and Adolfo Cova, host of a weekly radio program, have publicly accused the current and fourth Latino association (the MVLA) of not supporting their businesses, and others have felt that the association favored Dominicans. However, the MVLA, just as the previous organizations, is called upon by the media and local politicians to be the voice of the Hispanic community and has never shirked requests, in spite of the personal criticisms often directed at its leaders.

Religion is where many local Hispanics have found comfort and have directed much of their time and energy to help their churches thrive. The Catholic Church was an early supporter of the first Puerto Ricans in Utica, and the Diocese of Syracuse should be recognized for the creation of the Spanish Apostolate, the arrival of Milton Valladares and, subsequently, for the establishment of the Spanish Center and the first Latino association. Even up to the present day, Historic Old Saint John's Church offers a weekly mass in Spanish. Other churches, many with Spanish services and led by Hispanics, have also been formed. The Iglesia de Cristo Misionera (on Elizabeth Street) traces its roots to before the 1970s. One of its ministers, Rev. Antonia Cardona, published *Te veo luego*, a semi-autobiographical work that traces her spiritual journey after the tragic death of her daughter. Other Hispanic churches in the area include the Asamblea de Iglesias Cristianas (on Nichols Street), Faro de Luz Seventh Day Adventist Church (on Park Street), the Iglesia de Dios Altísimo (on Columbia Street) and the Iglesia Maranatha in Rome, NY.

Possibly the greatest achievement of Hispanics in the local area is their spectacular growth in numbers during the past fifty years. In spite of the closing factories and the decrease in Utica's population from approximately 100,000 in the 1960s to roughly 60,000 in recent years, Hispanics have continued to arrive in Utica, forming 13.6 percent of the city's population in 2015. Puerto Ricans have always constituted the majority of the Hispanic community. Since the decade of the 1990s, more Dominicans have arrived and form the second largest Hispanic nationality. This composition contrasts with the national Latino profile, where roughly two thirds are Mexican-Americans, which is the third largest Hispanic group in Utica. The local Latino community includes people from all Spanish-speaking countries, but those from the Caribbean dominate.

The first Puerto Ricans looked for jobs in the city's factories and slaughterhouses. As those jobs gradually went away, Puerto Ricans continued to arrive because the bad economic conditions in Utica were still better than those in Puerto Rico. In the early 1990s the Dominicans began to arrive. They were more interested in setting up their own businesses, which have helped to change the face of Utica. Thirty of the current forty Hispanic businesses in Utica are Dominican-owned and operated and include restaurants, small corner stores, barbershops, beauty salons, among others. These are small businesses, yet generate employment, and gladly serve both non-Hispanics and Hispanics, even though the Spanish language is usually present. Hispanics from New York City have been attracted to the area's lower cost of living and slower pace of life. Especially after the September 11 attacks, many more Hispanics began arriving in Utica, even during the hard times of the 2008-2009 economic crisis.

The story of Hispanics in Utica is certainly "a work in progress." The community still has challenges to face to improve its representation in the workforce and government, especially in elected office. The local Hispanic community is similar to the Italian immigrants who arrived in great numbers in the early twentieth century, constituting a linguistic mosaic of mutually incomprehensible Southern Italian dialects, with little uniting them except religion and birth in the same peninsula. Until the political maneuvering of Rufus Elefante helped the group gain a united voice, they were invisible politically, but they quickly realized that voting together would enable them to control the area's politics. Such a mobilization has not occurred among local Hispanics. Nevertheless, the group is finding success in making their lives in the area. Several people throughout the decades have tried to improve conditions for fellow Hispanics, such as Milton Valladares, Miguel Rivera, Miriam Rivera, Frank Calaprice, Santos Molina, Rafael Jiménez, Nelson Santiago, Sofia Novoa, Marilyn DeSuárez, Jorge Hernández, Tim Chavez, Mario Colón, Tony Colón, Sonia Martínez, and others. Success, though, can also be gauged by the ability to live in peace, to work, and to raise children to be productive citizens. Maria Santa Delgado was honored in the Upthegrove Memorial precisely for her selfless efforts as a single mother in raising a large family of children to successful careers. She indeed represents the average Hispanic who comes to Utica, silently working and improving the community, in order to make it a better place for generations of Uticans to come.

# ILLUSTRATIONS

Front Cover

    Couple at Mt. Carmel Festival. Photo by Larry Pacilio © 1975.

Chapter 1

    Map 1. Southeastern Oneida County. U.S. Census Bureau, 2010-2014 American Community Survey 5-Year Estimates.

    Map 2. The City of Utica. U.S. Census Bureau, 2010-2014 American Community Survey 5-Year Estimates.

Chapter 2

    Spanish Action League. *Observer-Dispatch* (O-D), August 10, 1969, p. 3B.

    Café Tropicano. Playing Dominos. Photo by Jim Armstrong. *O-D*, October 26, 1975, p. 1B.

    In Santos Molina's bodega. Photo by George Widman. *The Daily Press*, April 6, 1978, p. 1.

Chapter 3

    Miguel Rivera. Photo by Jim Armstrong. *O-D*, December 21, 1980, p. 3B.

    Elving Lagares. Photo by Mike Doherty. *The Sunday O-D*, December 6, 1981, p. 4A.

    La Posada 1981. Photo by Steve Roach. *The Daily Press*, December 21, 1981, p. 13.

    Patricia Chamberlain and Angelo Santiago. Photo by Mike Doherty. *The Sunday O-D*, December 6, 1981, p. 4A.

    UCAi Headstart Program. Photo by George Widman. *O-D*,

December 21, 1980, p. 3B.

Rafael Jiménez and Nelson Santiago. Photo by *O-D*, June 16, 1985, p. 5A

LAST helps Puerto Rico. *The Sunday O-D*, November 6, 1985, p. 1E.

La Posada 1980. Photo by Kay Arcuri. *O-D*, December 21, 1980, p. 3B.

Chapter 4

Hispanos Unidos. Photo by Gary Fountain, *O-D*, November 5,1992, p 5.

Clippings from El Despertar hispano americano:

Bethely Newman, "Maestros de Utica rompen la barrera lingüística." *O-D*, March 13, 1993, p. 1B.

Jorge Novillo, "Medios bilingües promueven integración cultural de los hispanos." *O-D*, February 27, 1993, p. 1B.

Salvador Pérez, "Un llamado por la unidad de los latinos." *O-D*, April 10, 1993, p. 1B.

Maritza Espinal, "Un calvario de abuela: Toño no volvió." *O-D*, March 27, 1993, p. 1B.

Tim Chavez, "Jugadores latinos encuentran un amigo en reportero del O-D." *O-D*, July 24, 1993, p. 1B.

Chapter 6

Erik Ortiz next to his newly painted storefront. Photo Elizabeth A. Mundshenk, *O-D*, September 14, 1995, p 1A.

Chapter 12

María Santa Rivera on the Rev. Franklin Upthegrove Memorial Wall, March 2017. Photo J. A. Fernández Canosa.

El Barajo Restaurant, February 2017. Photo by J. A. Thomas.

Chapter 13

Sonia Martínez. Photo, courtesy of Sonia Martínez.

Tony Colón. Photo, courtesy of Tony Colón.

Back Cover

Recreation of Erik Ortiz's Mural. Painting by Alexandra Almanzar.

# ACKNOWLEDGMENTS

Writing this book would not have been possible without the help of many people. Dr. Eugene Nassar not only first proposed the idea to me (along with Dr. Frank Bergmann) but also helped in its realization in very substantive ways. He even remembered where and when he saw the photo "Couple at Mt. Carmel Festival" (over forty years ago) and recommended it for the book's cover. After hearing my pleas for help regarding publishing, he interceded on my behalf with Dr. James Pula, who very graciously offered to format the book. Dr. Pula has dedicated a great deal of time toward the production of this volume, and his invaluable advice has improved the original manuscript.

I am grateful to *The Observer-Dispatch* for permission to cite published articles and to reproduce microfilm images of photos. Past *O-D* reporters and editors such as Tim Chavez and Jorge Hernández wrote passionately about the local Hispanic community, and this book cites much of their work. I thank Mr. David Dudajek, Opinion/Viewpoints Editor, and Mr. Ron Johns, Executive Editor, for their interest in this project and for their efforts in trying to locate some photos. The staff of the Utica College Library, including Jan Malcheski, Janis Winn, Lisa Rogers, Marie Iannone, Nancy Virgil-Call, and Herb LaGoy, has been helpful in many ways, especially with the microfilm reader. Utica College Research grants and fellowships have helped me throughout the years to present various stages of this project at several conferences, and a sabbatical leave granted by the College allowed for quality time to finish this book. I would also like to thank several donors who have recently given generous gifts to the Eugene Paul Nassar Ethnic Heritage Studies Center (EPNEHSC) in Dr. Nassar's memory.

I am indebted to Mr. Larry Pacilio for allowing his photograph to be used on the cover. The photo is stunning in its own right, but I hope it will encourage people to read the book, perhaps not to learn specific details about the couple depicted in the image but rather about the community that they represent. I also thank Mr. Michael Somple, Munson-Williams-Proctor Institute Art Registrar and Exhibition Manager, and Ms. Laura Laubenthal, Museum Assistant Registrar, for quickly locating and sending me a copy of the brochure about Larry Pacilio's exhibition in 1975. My thanks also go to my former student, Alexandra Almanzar, for recreating Erik Ortiz's mural, and for reading and commenting on the first draft. Dr. Jessica Gordon-Burroughs at Hamilton College and my father, Mr. Tom Thomas, also made helpful suggestions for the first chapters. A big thank you goes to Dr. Marie-Noëlle Little for her reading of the second draft and for a thorough list of suggestions, all of which enhanced the readability and scholarly level of this text. An equally big thanks goes to Dr. Frank Bergmann for his meticulous reading of the third draft and for his comments which helped clarify some ambiguous passages. I would also like to thank Dr. Bergmann for his support in guiding me through the workings of the EPNEHSC and providing direction when I had reached impasses.

Most importantly, without the input of the local Hispanic community this book could not have been written. I, therefore, thank all those who endured my long interviews and recordings, especially Sonia Martínez, Tony Colón, Mario Colón, Pedro Barajo Burdier, John Franco, and many others. This "diary" is a small first-step in describing the local Hispanic community, and I hope it will lead to further research.

# ENDNOTES

## INTRODUCTION

[1] James S. Pula, ed., *Ethnic Utica* (Utica: Oneida County Historical Society, 2002).

[2] Juan A. Thomas, "Language Selection by Hispanics in a Small Upstate New York Community," *Sociolinguistic Studies*, 6, 3, 2012, 571-593.

[3] Juan A. Thomas, "Watching the Development of U.S. Spanish: Data from a Small, Upstate City in New York," in Rudolf Muhr, et al., eds., *Exploring Linguistic Standards in Non-dominant Varieties of Pluricentric Languages/Explorando estándares lingüísticos en variedades no dominantes de lenguas pluricéntricas* (Frankfurt a.M./Wien u.a.: Peter Lang Verlag, 2013), 457-471.

[4] Juan A. Thomas, "What is Utica Spanish Like?" in Département de Linguistique de l'Université de Genève, ed., *Travaux du 19ème Congrès International des Linguistes* (Geneva, Switzerland. http://www.cil19.org/uploads/documents/What_is_Utica_Spanish_like.pdf, 2013.

[5] Juan A. Thomas, "Anglicismos en el español de Utica, New York: de la lengua hablada al diccionario/Anglicisms in the Spanish of Utica, NY: from the spoken language to the dictionary," *Glosas*, 2016, 9,1, 41-51.

[6] Juan A. Thomas, "In Search of a Standard: Spanish in a Small, Upstate N.Y. Community," in Rudolf Muhr, Dawn Marley, eds., *Pluricentric Languages: New Perspectives in Theory and Description* (Frankfurt a.M. /Wien u.a.: Peter Lang Verlag, 2015), 191-204.

## CHAPTER 1

[1] Sharon R. Ennis, Merarys Ríos-Vargas, and Nora G. Albert, *The Hispanic Population: 2010*, (C2010BR-04) U.S. Census Bureau, May 2011, 1.

[2] *Ibid.*, 3.

[3] *Ibid.*, 5.

[4] U.S. Census Bureau, *Notes on Estimates for Language Spoken at Home from the 2013 American Community Survey*. <http://www.census.gov/acs/www/downloads/user_notes/2013_language.pdf/> (Retrieved 26 October 2014), 4.

[5] Ray Wilkinson, "Un cadeau de la providence," *Réfugiés*, 2005, 138, 5-25.

[6] http://www.mla.org/cgi-shl/docstudio/docs.pl?map_data_results.

[7] Barbara Charzuk and Dean Toda, "Hispanics a Language Apart," *The Observer-Dispatch*, April 2, 1978, 1B-2B.

[8] Susan Tomer, "Utican's Puerto Ricans Fight for Existence," *O-D*, February 15, 1970, 2B.

[9] Debbie Groom, "Utica's Hispanic Mission Helps Preserve Spanish Culture," *The Daily Press*, June 2, 1984, 3.

[10] "Bishop Foery Names Spanish Director," *The Daily Press*, July 7, 1969, 21.

[11] Rocco Palladino, "St. John's the Real 'Amigo' to Utica's Spanish," *O-D*, August 10, 1969, 3B.

[12] Susan Tomer, *op. cit.*, 2B.

[13] *Ibid.*

[14] Antonia Rodríguez, "Utica Puerto Ricans Progressing, She Says," *O-D*, March 7, 1970.

[15] "Center to Present Spanish 'Treat,'" *O-D*, August 23, 1970, 2B; Mullin, Chet, "City's Spanish-Speaking Plan a Fiesta Sunday," *The Daily Press*, October 10, 1970, 6.

[16] "Center Sets 3-Day Spanish Festival," *The Daily Press*, September 24, 1971, 12.

[17] "Sons of Italy Plan Sunday March. Parade is Tribute to Columbus," *The Daily Press*, October 8, 1971, 20.

[18] "Christmas a la Latin," *O-D*, November 28, 1971, 2C.

[19] "Voice says Community Panel lacks Total Representation," *The Daily Press*, July 23, 1971, 12.

[20] Chet Mullin, "25 Picket School Board Over Member Appointment," *O-D*, July 23, 1971, 11.

[21] "Spanish Unit Backs Cutler, Upthegrove," *O-D*, 29 April 29, 1972, 3.

[22] Ernest Gray, "Neurologist Walks Out of Stormy Session," *Daily Sentinel*, September 2, 1971, 2.

[23] "UCAI Admits 2 Groups as Delegate Agencies," *The Daily Press*, January 25, 1972, 11.

[24] David Beatty, "OEO expected to cut funds to UCAI in '70," *O-D*, September 30, 1969, 17.

[25]"State of New York, Supreme Court, Oneida County (legal notice)," *O-D*, May 10, 1972, 32.

[26]Barbara Charzuk and Dean Toda, "Community Center: Congenial but Not Aggressive," *The Daily Press*, April 5, 1978, 1.

[27]"Action Center Aide Named," *The Observer-Dispatch*, April 19, 1972, 21.

[28]Susan Tomer, "UCAI Fiscal Exam Asked," *The Daily Press*, December 13, 1972, 23.

[29]Andrea Long, "Language Barrier: A Problem for Some," *O-D*, August 12, 1973, 5E.

[30]Matthew J. Dudek, "75 Utica Students Learn to Speak a 2nd Language," *O-D*, July 30, 1973, 11.

[31]Yolanda Jones, "Judges Approve Translator," *The Daily Press*, April 5, 1975, 7.

[32]Annette Jimenez, "Frank Calaprice Helps Utica's Hispanics Get Things Done," *O-D*, December 25, 1990, 3-4A.

[33]Herb Pinder, "'Frankito' Bridges Gap for Hispanic Community," *O-D*, December 19, 1985, 1B.

[34]"Utica College Spanish Dinner Set," *O-D*, May 12, 1970, 8.

[35]Yolanda Jones, *op. cit.*, 7.

[36]"Volunteers Honored," *O-D*, June 19, 1975, 27.

[37]"Big Picnic Planned by City Center," *O-D*, July 6, 1975, 3C.

[38]"A Time for Details," *O-D*, August 24, 1975, 4C; Jonas Kover, "Rhythm was Latin for 300," *O-D*, September 8, 1975, 7.

[39]Mark Patinkin, "Spanish-Speaking Job Seekers Find Language Barrier Biggest Problem," *O-D*, October 26, 1975, 1B, 6B

[40]Yolanda Jones, "Housing Leads Topics at 2nd Hearing," *The Daily Press*, February 10, 1976, 7.

[41]"Their Target is Food," *O-D*, December 18, 1976, 25.

[42]"Community Awards Presented," *O-D*, June 9, 1977, 19.

[43]Debbie Groom, *op. cit.*, 3.

[44]Phil Spartano, "1,500 Puerto Ricans Call Utica Home," *The Daily Press*, June 13, 1977.

[45]David E. Williams, "Hispanic Action League Meets to Reorganize," *O-D*, February 16, 1978, 13.

[46]Barbara Charzuk and Dean Toda, "Hispanics a Language Apart," *op. cit.* 1B-2B.

[47]Barbara Charzuk and Dean Toda, "Utica's Spanish Gather at Bleecker St. Grocery," *The Daily Press*, April 6, 1978, 1.

[48]*Ibid.*

[49]Barbara Charzuk and Dean Toda, "Hispanics a Language Apart," *op. cit.*, 2B.

[50]*Ibid.*

[51] Barbara Charzuk and Dean Toda, "Utica's Spanish Gather at Bleecker St. Grocery," *op. cit.*, 1.

[52] Barbara Charzuk and Dean Toda, "Spanish is Both a Tie and a Barrier," *The Daily Press,* April 3, 1978, 1.

[53] Barbara Charzuk and Dean Toda, "Hispanics a Language Apart," *op. cit.*, 2B.

[54] Barbara Charzuk and Dean Toda, "Utica's Spanish Cite Lack of Community Services," *The Daily Press*, April 4,1978, 1.

[55] Barbara Charzuk and Dean Toda, "Spanish is Both a Tie and a Barrier," *op. cit.,* 1, 7

[56] Barbara Charzuk and Dean Toda, "Utica's Spanish Cite Lack of Community Services," *op. cit.*, 1.

[57] Barbara Charzuk and Dean Toda, "Community Center: Congenial but Not Aggressive," *op. cit.*, 1.

[58] Barbara Charzuk and Dean Toda, "Utica's Spanish Cite Lack of Community Services," *op. cit.*, 1.

[59] Barbara Charzuk and Dean Toda, "Utica's Spanish Gather at Bleecker St. Grocery," *op. cit.*, 1.

[60] *Ibid.*

[61] Charzuk, Barbara and Dean Toda, "Community Center: Congenial but Not Aggressive," *op. cit.*, 1.

[62] *Ibid.*

[63] *Ibid.*

[64] Frank Calaprice, "Questions Series on Hispanics," *Daily Press*, April 15, 1978, 4.

## CHAPTER 2

[1] Barbara Charzuk and Dean Toda, "Hispanics a Language Apart," *The Observer-Dispatch(O-D)*, April 2, 1978, 1B-2B.

[2] Susan Tomer, "Utican's Puerto Ricans Fight for Existence," *O-D*, February 15, 1970, 2B.

[3] Debbie Groom, "Utica's Hispanic Mission Helps Preserve Spanish Culture,' *The Daily Press*, June 2, 1984, 3.

[4] "Bishop Foery Names Spanish Director," *The Daily Press*, July 7, 1969, 21.

[5] Rocco Palladino, "St. John's the Real 'Amigo' to Utica's Spanish,' *O-D*, August 10, 1969, 3B.

[6] Susan Tomer, *op. cit.*, 2B.

[7] *Ibid.*

[8] Antonia Rodríguez, "Utica Puerto Ricans Progressing, She Says," *O-D*, March 7, 1970.

[9]"Center to Present Spanish 'Treat,'" *O-D*, August 23, 1970, 2B; Mullin, Chet, "City's Spanish-Speaking Plan a Fiesta Sunday," *The Daily Press*, October 10, 1970, 6.

[10]"Center Sets 3-Day Spanish Festival," *The Daily Press*, September 24, 1971, 12.

[11]"Sons of Italy Plan Sunday March. Parade is Tribute to Columbus," *The Daily Press*, October 8, 1971, 20.

[12]"Christmas a la Latin," *O-D*, November 28, 1971, 2C.

[13]"Voice Says Community Panel Lacks Total Representation," *The Daily Press*, July 23, 1971, 12.

[14]Chet Mullin, "25 Picket School Board Over Member Appointment" *O-D*, July 23, 1971, 11.

[15]"Spanish Unit Backs Cutler, Upthegrove,'" *O-D*, April 29, 1972, 3.

[16]Ernest Gray, "Neurologist Walks Out of Stormy Session," *Daily Sentinel*, September 2, 1971, 2.

[17]"UCAI Admits 2 Groups as Delegate Agencies," *The Daily Press*, January 25, 1972, 11.

[18]David Beatty, "OEO Expected to Cut Funds to UCAI in '70," *O-D*, September 30, 1969, 17.

[19]"State of New York, Supreme Court, Oneida County (legal notice)," *O-D*, May 10, 1972, 32.

[20]Barbara Charzuk and Dean Toda, "Community Center: Congenial but Not Aggressive," *The Daily Press*, April 5, 1978, 1.

[21]"Action Center Aide Named," *The Observer-Dispatch*, April 19, 1972, 21.

[22]Susan Tomer, "UCAI Fiscal Exam Asked," *The Daily Press*, December 13, 1972, 23.

[23]Andrea Long, "Language Barrier: A Problem for Some," *O-D*, August 12, 1973, 5E.

[24]Matthew J. Dudek, "75 Utica Students Learn to Speak a 2nd Language," *O-D*, July 30, 1973, 11.

[25]Yolanda Jones, "Judges Approve Translator," *The Daily Press*, April 5, 1975, 7.

[26]Annette Jimenez, "Frank Calaprice Helps Utica's Hispanics Get Things Done," *O-D*, December 25, 1990, 3-4A.

[27]Herb Pinder, "'Frankito' Bridges Gap for Hispanic Community," *O-D*, December 19, 1985, 1B.

[28]"Utica College Spanish Dinner Set," *O-D*, May 12, 1970, 8.

[29]Yolanda Jones, *op. cit.*, 7.

[30]"Volunteers honored," *O-D*, June 19, 1975, 27.

[31]"Big Picnic Planned by City Center," *O-D*, July 6, 1975, 3C.

[32]"A Time for Details," *O-D*, August 24, 1975, 4C; Jonas Kover, "Rhythm was Latin for 300," *O-D*, September 8, 1975, 7.

[33] Mark Patinkin, "Spanish-Speaking Job Seekers Find Language Barrier Biggest Problem," *O-D*, October 26, 1975, 1B, 6B

[34] Yolanda Jones, "Housing Leads Topics at 2nd Hearing," *The Daily Press*, February 10, 1976, 7.

[35] "Their Target is Food," *O-D*, December 18, 1976, 25.

[36] "Community Awards Presented,' *O-D*, June 9, 1977, 19.

[37] Debbie Groom, *op. cit.*, 3.

[38] Phil Spartano, "1,500 Puerto Ricans Call Utica Home," *The Daily Press*, June 13, 1977.

[39] David E. Williams, "Hispanic Action League Meets to Reorganize," *O-D*, February 16, 1978, 13.

[40] Barbara Charzuk and Dean Toda, "Hispanics a Language Apart," *op. cit.* 1B-2B.

[41] Barbara Charzuk and Dean Toda, "Utica's Spanish Gather at Bleecker St. Grocery," *The Daily Press*, April 6, 1978, 1.

[42] *Ibid.*

[43] Barbara Charzuk and Dean Toda, "Hispanics a Language Apart," *op. cit.*, 2B.

[44] *Ibid.*

[45] Barbara Charzuk and Dean Toda, "Utica's Spanish Gather at Bleecker St. Grocery," *op. cit.*, 1.

[46] Barbara Charzuk and Dean Toda, "Spanish is Both a Tie and a Barrier," *The Daily Press,* April 3, 1978, 1.

[47] Barbara Charzuk and Dean Toda, "Hispanics a Language Apart," *op. cit.*, 2B.

[48] Barbara Charzuk and Dean Toda, "Utica's Spanish Cite Lack of Community Services," *The Daily Press*, April 4,1978, 1.

[49] Barbara Charzuk and Dean Toda, "Spanish is Both a Tie and a Barrier," *op. cit.,* 1, 7.

[50] Barbara Charzuk and Dean Toda, "Utica's Spanish Cite Lack of Community Services," *op. cit.*, 1.

[51] Barbara Charzuk and Dean Toda, "Community Center: Congenial but not Aggressive," *op. cit.*, 1.

[52] Barbara Charzuk and Dean Toda, "Utica's Spanish Cite Lack of Community Services," *op. cit.*, 1.

[53] Barbara Charzuk and Dean Toda, "Utica's Spanish Gather at Bleecker St. Grocery," *op. cit.*, 1.

[54] *Ibid.*

[55] Barbara Charzuk and Dean Toda, "Community Center: Congenial but not Aggressive," *op. cit.*, 1.

[56] *Ibid.*

[57] *Ibid.*

[58] Frank Calaprice, "Questions Series on Hispanics," *Daily Press*, April 15, 1978, 4.

# CHAPTER 3

[1] Don Knorr, "Puerto Rican Community an Island Unto Itself," *O-D*, December 21, 1980, 1B, 3B.

[2] Morris Brown, "Minority Officers Few Despite Area's Efforts," *O-D*, June 25, 1981, 17.

[3] *Ibid.*

[4] *Ibid.*

[5] Tim Rice, "Hispanics Believe Children Real Hope," *The Sunday O-D*, December 6, 1981 1A, 4A.

[6] *Ibid.*

[7] Tim Rice, "'Spanish Center' Mainstream Link," *The Sunday O-D*, December 6, 1981, 4A.

[8] Tim Rice, "I make Out, But It's Tough," *The Sunday O-D*, December 6, 1981, 4A.

[9] Tim Rice, "For Hispanics, Christmas Festive With Food, Music," *O-D*, December 21, 1981, 1, 12.

[10] Debbie Groom, "Christmas Festivity Re-enacted," *The Daily Press,* December 21, 1981, 13.

[11] Marj Patrick, "Hispanics Return Favor: Community Battles for Interpreter to Keep Her Job," *The Daily Press*, March 25, 1982.

[12] Tim Rice, "Hispanics Sign Petition To Keep Interpreter," *O-D*, March 29, 1982, 11.

[13] Tim Rice, "Hispanics Ask Mayor To Discuss Problems of Courts, Layoffs," *O-D*, March 23, 1982, 15.

[14] *Ibid.*

[15] Marj Patrick, "Mayor Gives Pledge: Says He'll Name Hispanic to Fire Department," *The Daily Press*, March 14, 1982

[16] Tim Rice, "Hispanics Sign Petition To Keep Interpreter," *op. cit.*, 11.

[17] "Hispanics Want UCAI Job Saved," *The Daily Press*, April 6, 1982, 3.

[18] Marj Patrick, "UCAI Losing Staff, Centers, Programs, But It's 'No Titanic,'" *The Daily Press*, July 27, 1982, 6.

[19] Mike Houston, "Policeman Calls His Release Unjustifiable," *The Daily Press*, June 21, 1984, 9.

[20] Kathy Shwiff, "Discrimination Complaint Names City," *The Daily Press*, August 14, 1984, 6.

[21] "Commission Dismisses Complaint," *O-D*, August 29, 1984, 15.

[22] Edwin Darden and Matthew Worth, "Jury Duty: Who Gets Called?" *O-D*, January 18, 1987, 1D.

[23] Herb J. Pinder, "Hiring imbalance," *O-D*, February 10, 1985, 1-2C.

[24] Herb J. Pinder, "When Their Language is a Barrier," *The Sunday O-D*, February 17, 1985, 2B.

[25] Herb J. Pinder, "Officials Say There're Seldom Any Problems," *The Sunday O-D*, February 17, 1985, 2B.

[26] Don Knorr, "There's Hope Peeking Out From Empty Store Fronts," *The Sunday O-D*, June 15, 1985, 4-5A.

[27] *Ibid.*, 5A.

[28] Herb J. Pinder, "L.A.S.T. Hopes to Grow," *O-D*, February 12, 1984, B1.

[29] Don Knorr, "Little Progress Seen by Hispanics," *O-D*, April 26, 1983, 18.

[30] Don Knorr, "New Voices, New Attitudes Speak a Language of Unity," *The Sunday O-D*, June 15, 1985, 1A, 5A.

[31] Don Knorr, "Hispanic Dance Steps Toward Latin Unity," *O-D*, February 10, 1985, 1C.

[32] Editor O-D, "Drive for Hispanic Unity is Important Effort," *O-D*, June 19, 1985, 6.

[33] Don Knorr, "New Voices, New Attitudes Speak a Language of Unity," *op. cit.*, 5A.

[34] Tom Cocola, "Hispanic Group Seeks Funds for Heritage Carnival," *The Daily Press*, August 14, 1985, 3.

[35] Brandon Craig, "L.A.S.T.'s First Festival Called a Success," *The Daily Press*, September 16, 1985, 7.

[36] Sylvia Rainford, "Dispute Leads to 2 Hispanic Beauty Titles," *The O-D*, October 2, 1985, 13.

[37] Sylvia Rainford, "Hispanic Title Goes to Irizarry," *O-D*, October 6, 1985, 1B.

[38] Don Knorr, "MVCC Freshman is Named Miss Hispanic of Utica," *O-D*, November 2, 1985, 1C.

[39] Bill Farrell, "Help Is On the Way: L.A.S.T. Aiding Puerto Rican Flood Victims," *The Sunday O-D*, November 24, 1985, E1.

[40] "Puerto Rico Seeking Federal Disaster Aid," *O-D*, October 9, 1985, 1.

[41] Don Knorr, "Some Hispanics Await Word While Others Breathe Easier," *O-D*, October 9, 1985, 1.

[42] Edwin Darden, "Council Candidate Raps Ballot Placement; Says it Cost Him," *The Daily Press*. November 7, 1985, 12.

[43] Don Knorr, "Minority Candidates Continue to Struggle: Hispanics Still Aim for Council," *O-D*, November 10 1985, B1, B3.

[44] Shirley Williams, "'Tis the Season for Helping," *O-D*, December 21, 1986, 1D.

[45] "Colón Out of Race for 116th," *O-D*, May 19, 1986, 9.

[46] Jonas Kover, "Latin Festival Joining Summer Time," *The Daily Press*, July 10, 1986, 3.

[47]Dave Dudajek, "Good Friday is Special to Hispanics," *The Sunday O-D*, April 3, 1988, 1E, 3E.

[48]Ramona Whitehurst, "Dinner Will Highlight Month for Hispanics," *O-D*, September 24, 1989, 4B

[49]Dave Dudajek, "A Hero at Home in Community," *O-D*, September 28, 1989, 1C, 5C.

[50]David Dupont, "Forum Focuses on Hispanic Success Stories," *O-D* September 23, 1989, 3A, 6A.

# CHAPTER 4

[1]Mike Houston, "First Hispanic named to major Utica panel," *O-D*, January 4, 1990, 3A.

[2]Victor Andino, "Utica teacher Rivera gives lesson in self-esteem," *O-D*, August 30, 1992, 3A.

[3]Debbie Groom, "Utica area in salute to '*Longaniza,*'" *O-D*, August 16, 1992, 9B.

[4]Dave Dudajek, "Faces in the crowd," *O-D*, December 30, 1995, 1C.

[5]Sofia Novoa, "Survey hopes to assess the needs of Hispanics/ Encuesta busca determinar necesidades," *O-D*, May 29, 1993, 1B.

[6]Brian Sanger, "New group founded to help Hispanic community," *O-D*, November 5, 1992, 5.

[7]Joe Kelly, "I'm used to the noise," *O-D*, February 16, 1986, 1 -2E.

[8]Sofia Novoa, "Lack of services in Spanish main problem for Hispanics/Falta de servicios en español problema para los Hispanos," *O-D*, April 2, 1994, 1B.

[9]David Pace, "Hispanics own potential political clout," *O-D*, August 26, 2001, 4A.

[10]Kelly Hassett, "Minority growth not reflected in political campaigns," *O-D*, August 27, 2001, 1B.

[11]Kimberly Taylor, "Hispanic culture attuned to 'With You on Saturday,'" *O-D*, March 31, 1992, 3A.

[12]Girard Plante, "Area listeners love Polish, Spanish, Italian flavor," *O-D*, January 9, 1993, 1B, 3B.

[13]"Hispanics seek positive area identity/Hispanos quieren identidad positiva," *O-D*, January 16, 1993, 1A.

[14]Elizabeth Spraker, "Chocolate's rich history originated in celebrations of Mexico/Rica historia de chocolate se originó en celebraciones mexicanas," *O-D*, February, 13 1993, 1B.

[15]Fabián Ramírez, "Puerto Rico Island seeking its destiny/ Puerto Rico Isla buscando destino," *O-D*, July 10, 1993, 1B.

[16] *op. cit.* "Teaching child two languages makes her world richer/Enseñar a niño dos lenguas enriquece su mundo," *O-D*, January 16, 1993, 1B.

[17] Maritza Espinal, "Kindergarten special time with special teacher/Jardín de infancia ofrece experiencias especiales," *O-D*, June 26, 1993, 1B.

[18] Maritza Espinal, "We long for the innocence, simplicity of Mother's Day/Anhelamos la inocencia, sencillez del Día de la Madre," *O-D*, May 15, 1993, 1B.

[19] Maritza Espinal, "A grandmother's calvary: Toño did not return/Un calvario de abuela: Toño no volvió," *O-D*, March 27, 1993, 1B.

[20] Elizabeth Spraker, "Drugs prey on Hispanics here and in Latin America/Las drogas abaten a los hispanos aquí," *O-D*, June 12, 1993, 1B.

[21] Josefina Bonilla-Grasso, "Open your mind and heart to person, not appearance/Abre la mente, corazón a la persona, no la apariencia," *O-D*, April 24, 1993, 1B.

[22] Salvador Pérez, "Conference stresses need for Latinos to unite/ Un llamado por la unidad de los latinos," *O-D*, April 10, 1993, 1B.

[23] Elizabeth Spraker, "Las necesidades de los latinos según su crecimiento/Needs of Latinos grow," *O-D*, August 7, 1993, 1B.

[24] Tim Chavez, "Objeto: Rompiendo barreras/Conference goal: Breaking barriers," *O-D*, October 27, 1993, 3A.

[25] *op. cit.* "A new sunrise/Un nuevo amanecer," *O-D*, November 27, 1993, 1B.

[26] Tim Chavez, "Focus on nation's Hispanic kids," *O-D*, February, 16, 1998, 7A.

[27] Rick Jensen, "New face, same tradition of community service," *O-D*, September 22, 1996, 6B.

[28] Tim Chavez, "Hispanics seek recognition throughout heritage month," *O-D*, October 6, 1997, 7A.

[29] *Ibid.*

[30] Jorge Hernández, "Spanish Heritage Month is a time for learning," *O-D*, October 1, 1996, 8A.

[31] Jorge Hernández, "Teaching diversity in language classes," *O-D*, December 17, 1995, 8A.

[32] *op. cit.* "Spanish Heritage Month is a time for learning," *O-D*, October 1, 1996, 8A.

[33] Jorge L. Hernández, "No apologies for name, by George," *O-D*, December 16, 1997, 9A.

[34] *Ibid.*

[35] Jorge Hernández, "Trip to Spain broadened youths' view of the world," *O-D*, June 10, 1998, 5B.

[36] Scott Wallace, "Utica reporter learns the duties of his job in Latin America," *O-D*, January 18, 1998, 1G.

[37] Patrick Gannon, "El Salvador rich in faith," *O-D*, January 6, 2002, 1G, 2G.

[38] Patrick Gannon, "People of El Salvador support U.S. in terrorism fight," *O-D*, January 6, 2002, 1G.

## CHAPTER 5

[1] Juan A. Thomas, *op. cit.*, *Sociolinguistic Studies*, 6,3, 2012, 571-593.

[2] Interview with Emily Powell, September 7, 2010.

[3] Interview with Román Santos, April 4, 2011.

[4] Maritza Espinal, "Teaching child two languages makes her world richer/Enseñar a niño dos lenguas enriquece su mundo," *O-D*, January 16, 1993, 1B.

[5] Interview with Pablo Balarezo, April 25, 2011.

[6] Jorge Novillo, "Parents struggle, strive for a better future for kids/Padres luchan por procurar un futuro mejor para sus hijos," *O-D*, January 30, 1993, 1B, 4B.

[7] Interview with Marna Solete, February 25, 2011.

[8] Interview with Pablo Balarezo, April 25, 2011.

[9] Tim Chavez, "Latino players find 'friend' in new O-D sports reporter/Jugadores latinos encuentran un amigo en reportero del O-D," *O-D*, July 24, 1993, 1B.

[10] Rafael Hermoso, "Baseball, a long way away," *O-D*, September 2, 1993, 1C, 4C.

[11] Lauren Gaddie, "Adjusting to America," *O-D*, August 20, 1997, 1C, 3C.

[12] Jorge Novillo, *op. cit.*, *O-D*, January 30, 1993, 1B, 4B.

[13] Jorge Novillo, "Bilingual offerings are moving Hispanics into the mainstream/Medios bilingües promueven integración cultural de los hispanos," *O-D*, February 27, 1993, 1B.

[14] Bethely Newman, "Utica teachers break the language barrier/Maestros de Utica rompen la barrera lingüística," *O-D*, March 13, 1993, 1B.

[15] Tim Chavez, "Losing language steals part of self," *O-D*, August 31, 1998, 7A.

[16] Kelly Hasset, "Spanish, Russian, Bosnian spoken here," *O-D*, May 24, 2002, 7A.

[17] Cassaundra Baber, "A growing need for court interpreters in area," *O-D*, February 24, 2011.
[18] *Ibid.*
[19] Chinki Sinha, "One woman's story: No English, tough times," *O-D*, December 27, 2007, 1A.
[20] Emerson Clarridge, "Police coax man down from Kennedy Plaza rooftop," *O-D*, August 7, 2009.
[21] Elena Rios, "Better health for Hispanics tonic for all," *O-D*, September 4, 2000, 7A.
[22] Denise-Marie Balona, "Cancer rates high in Latinas," *O-D*, September 27, 1999, 8B.
[23] Leha Byrd, "Minorities are misinformed about AIDS, HIV, survey says," *O-D*, December 1, 2000, 1A, 2A.
[24] LaVera Crawley, "Doctors, patients bridging the cultural divide," *O-D*, October 28, 2001, 1G, 2G.
[25] Bill Farrell, "Language barrier can add to Hispanics' health costs, *O-D*, October 29, 1993, 1-2A.
[26] Steve Frohnhoefer, "Medical interpreters answer growing need," *O-D*, June 15, 1998, 1B.
[27] Marrecca Fiore, "Area interpreters make new world less intimidating for immigrants," *O-D*, February 25, 2001, 1B, 3B.
[28] *Ibid.*
[29] Courtney Potts, "Refugees from around globe spur demand for medical interpreters," *O-D*, December 3, 2009.
[30] Bill Farrell, "UC aims to attract minority nurses," *O-D*, May 25, 2002, 1-2A.

# CHAPTER 6

[1] Tim Chavez, "Don't blame everything on Latinos in America," *O-D* September 15, 1995, 11A.
[2] Russ Davis, "Demand city do right in Ortiz outrage," *O-D*, September 19, 1995, 6A.
[3] *Ibid.*
[4] Lorna McNeill, "City paints over clothing store's mural," *O-D*, September 14, 1995, 1A, 7A.
[5] *Ibid.*, 1A.
[6] Lorna McNeill, "Hispanic community upset with Yacco," *O-D*, September 15, 1995, 1-2A.
[7] *Ibid.*, 2A.
[8] Lorna McNeill, "Mayoral candidates get involved with mural controversy," *O-D*, September 16, 1995, 3A.
[9] Tim Chavez, "Racism no longer an LA thing," *O-D*, September 17, 1995, 8B.

[10] op. cit., "Demand city do right in Ortiz outrage," *O-D*, September 19, 1995, 6A.

[11] *Ibid.*

[12] Pat Yacco, "Yacco says he didn't order mural covered up," *O-D*, September 1995.

[13] Alan D. Crockett, "Mural supporters plan protest of repainting," *O-D*, September 19, 1995, 3A.

[14] Alan Crockett, "Mural supporters picket," *O-D*, September 20, 1995, 3A.

[15] Suzanne King, "Marchers deliver messages of racial unity, mutual respect," *O-D*, September 22, 1995, 3A.

[16] Tim Chavez, "Utica's people of color must not battle," *O-D*, September 21, 1995, 10A.

[17] Louis LaPolla, "LaPolla defends city's actions," *O-D*, September 21, 1995, 11A.

[18] *Ibid.*

[19] Edward A. Hanna, "Hanna says city acted wrong," *O-D*, September 21, 1995, 11A.

[20] Alan Crockett, "Hispanics question Yacco," *O-D*, September 21, 1995, 3A.

[21] Juan Antonio Sánchez, "Erasing mural an insult to Spanish community," *O-D*, September 19, 1995, 6A.

[22] op.cit. "Hispanics question Yacco," *O-D*, September 21, 1995, 3A.

[23] Tim Chavez, "Minorities must first take down their walls to others," *O-D*, September 24, 1995, 9B.

[24] Alan D. Crockett, "Utica codes head under fire," *O-D*, September 25, 1995, 1A.

[25] "Hanna: pornographic computer program a reason to fire Saafir," *O-D*, September 25, 1995, 2A.

[26] Alan D. Crockett, "Saafir said he responded to concerns of residents when he painted over mural," *O-D*, September 25, 1995, 2A.

[27] R. Patrick Corbett, "Utica settles '95 ethnic mural case," *O-D*, June 9, 1999, 1B.

[28] Interview with John Franco, November 22, 2016.

## Chapter 7

[1] Lorna McNeill, "Bridge Building Coalition backs codes commissioner," *O-D*, October 22, 1995, 3A.

[2] Stephen F. Szmurlo, "Area rallies against racism," *O-D*, October 28, 1995, 3A.

[3] Bill Farrell, "Data say minorities get stiffer sentences," *O-D*, March 24, 1996, 1A, 5A.

[4] *Ibid.*, 5A.

[5] "Latinos raise voice in D.C. rally," *O-D*, October 13, 1996, 1A.

[6] Jorge Hernández, "Nurturing Latino futures," *O-D*, March 4, 1998, 5B.

[7] Arlene Levinson, "Black? White? Asian? Indian? Hispanic?," *O-D*, October 5, 1998, 13A.

[8] Tim Chavez, "Columbus' conquest still remains today," *O-D*, October 13, 1997, 7A.

[9] Editor, "Share in region's diversity," *O-D*, October 8, 1997.

[10] "All must celebrate diversity," *O-D*, October 16, 1997.

[11] Matt Leingang, "Proctor tries to ease ethnic tensions," *O-D*, March 17, 1998, 1B.

[12] Jorge Hernández, "Talking can take edge off animosity," *O-D*, March 20, 1998, 9A.

[13] *Ibid.*

[14] Dave Dudajek, "Message of unity grows at Proctor," *O-D*, May 1, 1998, 9A.

[15] *Ibid.*

[16] Gannett News Service, "Ingredients in America's melting pot slowly shifting," *O-D*, May 3, 1998, 1A.

[17] Marjorie Valbrun, "A wave of refugees lubricates rusty economy of Utica, N.Y.," *The Wall Street Journal*, March 8, 1999, 1.

[18] *Ibid.*

[19] *Ibid.*

[20] Kelly Hassett, "Refugees blend rich past, hopeful future in Utica," *O-D*, November 21, 1999, 1A, 9A.

[21] Diane Washington, "Education, relationships key to easing racial tension," *O-D*, March 23, 1999, 1B, 3B.

[22] *Ibid.*, 1B.

[23] *Ibid.*, 3B.

[24] Jim Specht, "Hispanics. More opportunities coming," *O-D*, July 5, 1998, 8A.

[25] Megan Allen, "Bridge Builders help ease tensions at Proctor," *O-D*, April 11, 2000, 3A.

[26] Jorge Hernández, "Door not closed on racial prejudice," *O-D*, July 11, 2002, 11A.

# CHAPTER 8

[1] Gannett News, "Hispanics No. 1 minority among kids," *O-D*, July 2, 1996, 1A.

[2] Lorna McNeill, "Area Hispanics seek respect," *O-D*, September 26, 1995, 1-2A.

[3] Jonas Kover, "Hispanic gala is more than just a dance," *O-D*, October 12, 1995, 1C.

[4] John Kohlstrand, "Region gets older, more diverse," *O-D*, December 18, 1997, 1A.

[5] Hector Cantu, "Hispanic market grows in size, importance," *O-D*, August 16, 1998, 1F.

[6] Mike Kilian, "Region's population falls, but count could be off," *O-D*, July 2, 1999, 1A.

[7] Kelly Hassett, "Refugees blend rich past, hopeful future in Utica," *O-D*, November 21, 1999, 1A, 9A.

[8] Brad Heath, "Region's shrinking population gets poorer," *O-D*, December 3, 1999, 1A, 11A.

[9] The Associated Press, "Census: Poverty rate 15.4 percent," *O-D*, December 20, 2001, 10A.

[10] Ellyn Ferguson, "Census Bureau mobilizes to minimize undercount," *O-D*, July 11, 1999, 5E.

[11] Steve Frohnhoefer, "Utica, region stand up to be counted in 2000," *O-D*, December 16, 1999, 1A, 3A.

[12] Steve Frohnhoeffer, "Census forms not as taxing as you think," *O-D*, March 19, 2000, 1A, 3A.

[13] Steve Frohnhoefer, "Area census response lags," *O-D*, April 8, 2000, 1B.

[14] Steve Frohnhoeffer, "Census returns: Oneida County stumbles," *O-D*, April 21, 2000, 1B.

[15] Steve Frohnhoeffer, "Students swell census count," *O-D*, March 22, 2000, 1B.

[16] Sergio Bustos and Deborah Mathis, "Hispanics reshape U.S.," *O-D*, July 2, 2000, 1A, 10A.

[17] Ellyn Ferguson, "Census Bureau created the term 'Hispanic,'" *O-D*, July 3, 2000, 4A.

[18] Tony Pugh, "Census: American Hispanics nearly as numerous as blacks," *O-D*, March 8, 2001, 1-2A.

[19] Tony Pugh, "Almost 7 million Americans multiracial," *O-D*, March 13, 2001, 5A.

[20] The Associated Press, "Census: Population gap between men and women narrow," *O-D*, September 10, 2001, 2A.

[21] Erika Rosenberg, "Diversity propels New York's growth," *O-D*, March 18, 2001, 9A.

[22] R. Patrick Corbett, "Region's head count confirms sharp loss," *O-D*, March 16, 2001, 1A, 6A.

[23] Erika Rosenberg, "Oneida County had nation's 12th biggest population loss in nation," *O-D*, April 3, 2001, 1B.

[24] Kelly Hassett, "Oneida Co. posts big gains in Hispanics and Asians," *O-D*, March 16, 2001, 6A.

[25] *Ibid.*

[26] Sergio Bustos, "U.S. Hispanics more diverse," *O-D*, May 10, 2001, 1-2A.

[27] Kelly Hassett, "Puerto Ricans, Vietnamese more common in region," *O-D*, May 22, 2001, 6A.

[28] Kelly Hassett, "Area remains segregated despite its racial, ethnic diversity," *O-D,* May 27, 2001, 1A.

[29] "Diversity numbers deceiving," *O-D*, May 27, 2001, 6D.

[30] Mary Marchio, "Prison population influences Hispanic count in Marcy," *O-D*, May 27, 2001, 5D.

[31] Marline Vargas-Rivera, "Hispanics in Marcy diversify culture," *O-D*, June 3, 2001, 6B.

[32] Editor, "Include minorities in region's life," *O-D*, June 3, 2001, 4B.

[33] Kelly Hassett, "Region struggles with integration," *O-D*, May 27, 2001, 4D.

[34] Jessica Guynn, "Latino workers courted by corporate America," *O-D*, October 9, 2001, 3D.

[35] Carrie Mason-Draffen, "Minority women own more firms," *O-D*, August 11, 1997, 5A.

[36] Marrecca Fiore, "Minorities feel punch of layoffs, recession," *O-D*, February 17, 2002 1B, 3B.

[37] David Alandete, "La población española se sextuplica en EEUU en la última década," *El País*, May 27, 2011.

[38] Hope Yen, "New census milestone: Hispanics reach 50 million in U.S." *O-D*, March 24, 2011.

[39] U.S. Census Bureau, "American Fact Finder. Profile of General Population and Housing Characteristics. Oneida County, New York," retrieved May 10, 2011.

[40] Elizabeth Cooper, "Region's diversity increasing, according to Census figures," *O-D*, March 26, 2011.

# Chapter 9

[1] Editor, "LaPolla's legacy richer with diversity," *O-D*, November 27, 1995, 6A.

[2] Editor, "Diversity must be key to stronger community," *O-D*, December 16, 2016, A16.

[3] Alan D. Crockett, "Face of workplace is colored white," *O-D*, December 17, 1995, 1A, 10A.

[4] Alan D. Crockett, "Satisfaction not guaranteed," *O-D*, December 17, 1995, 11A.

[5] Judy Manzer, "Minority deputies sought," *O-D*, March 13, 1999, 1A.

[6] Judy Manzer, "Few minorities in sheriff's department," *O-D*, April 18, 1999, 1A, 9A.

[7] *Ibid.*, 9A.

[8] *Ibid.*, 9A.

[9] Patrick Gannon, "Minorities few in county workplace," *O-D*, April 22, 2002, 1A, 6A.

[10] Alan D. Crockett, "Recruitment headache," *O-D*, December 18, 1995, 1A, 9A.

[11] Ken Little, "Women, minorities slowly change face of public safety," *O-D*, February 9, 2001, 1A, 8A.

[12] Rocco LaDuca, "Minorities, Utica police examine relationship in wake of Missouri shooting," *O-D*, September 7, 2014.

[13] Ned Campbell, "Speak Spanish? Rome police have a job for you," *O-D*, September 14, 2013.

[14] Editor, "Diversity needed in government," *O-D*, December 26, 1996, 10A.

[15] Ron Kampeas, "Statistics show minorities losing out on promotions," *O-D*, July 17, 2001, 5A.

[16] Rosenberg, Erika, "N.Y. Hispanics are voting more," *O-D*, July 26, 2000, 1B.

[17] Norma Sengupta, "Mario Colón: candidate 5th ward," *Utica Phoenix*, September 2009, 18, 24.

[18] Keshia Clukey, "6 vie for 2 Utica school board seats," *O-D*, May 17, 2013.

[19] S. Alexander Gerould, "Martínez looks to support Latinos," *O-D*, December 12, 2016, A3.

[20] United States Department of Justice, "Owner Of Utica Dog Food Plant Admits To Harboring Illegal Aliens," https://www.justice.gov/usao-ndny/pr/owner-utica-dog-food-plant-admits-harboring-illegal-aliens, 6 March 2017.

[21] David Sommerstien and Julia Botero, "Hispanic dairy workers step out of the shadows to protest abuses," https://www.northcountrypublicradio.org/news/story/28271/20150506/hispanic-dairy-workers-step-out-of-the-shadows-to-protest-abuses, 8 March 2017.

[22] Sarah Haase and Jennifer Edwards, "MVCC names first Hispanic trustee," *O-D*, January 21, 2009.

[23] Lorna McNeil, "Lack of minority teachers a lesson in black & white," *O-D*, December 19, 1995, 1A, 9A.

[24] Matt Leingang, "Utica lags in minority teachers," *O-D*, May 4, 1998, 1A.

[25] Diane Washington, "Utica schools offer plan to hire more minorities," *O-D*, October 6, 1998, 1A, 2A.

[26] Jennifer Smith, "Grant earmarked for recruiting minority teachers in Utica schools," *O-D*, January 26, 2002, 1A, 10A.

[27] Editor, "Diversity must be key to stronger community," *O-D*, December 18, 2016, A16-A17.

[28] Alissa Scott, "Study: Minority students on rise," *O-D*, December 16, 2016, A1, A4.

# CHAPTER 10

[1] Valorie Tramm Claburn, "Students leap the language hurdle," *O-D*, June 10, 1997, 1A, 2A.

[2] Femi Lewis, "Refugees eagerly learn English," *O-D*, August 4, 2000, 1B.

[3] Stefanie Scarlett, "Columbus School students discover America's diversity," *O-D*, October 12, 1998, 1A, 2A.

[4] Megan Allen, "Cultures blend in Utica schools," *O-D*, December 12, 1999, 1A, 4A.

[5] Jennifer Smith, "Teaching English year-round effort," *O-D*, July 5, 2001, 1A, 2A.

[6] Jennifer Warnick and Jennifer Smith, "Enrollment up in Utica City School District," *O-D*, September 20, 2001, 1B.

[7] *Ibid.*, 4A.

[8] Lorna McNeill, "'91 audit charged Utica schools with biased behaviors, attitudes," *O-D*, December 1995, 8A.

[9] Russ Davis, "Proctor's black Regents diploma rate 'appalling,'" *O-D*, September 12, 1999, 7B.

[10] *Ibid.*, 7B.

[11] Richard Whitmire, "Study: High dropout rate for Hispanics still puzzles researchers," *O-D*, August 6, 1997, 5A.

[12]Russ Davis, "Black students left behind," *O-D*, February 13, 2000, 1B, 3B.

[13]Michael Gormley, "Fourth-grade test scores improve around state, for minorities too," *O-D*, May 17, 2001 3A.

[14]Jennifer Smith and Bill Farrell, "English scores climb in area schools," *O-D*, May 17, 2001 1A, 3A.

[15]Jennifer Smith, "Language skills factor in success," *O-D*, March 28, 2002, 1A, 6A.

[16]Jennifer Smith, "Utica schools proud as test scores rise," *O-D*, March 28, 2002, 6A.

[17]Yancey Roy, "Report: Minorities have higher college dropout rate," *O-D*, November 1, 1996, 1B.

[18]"SUNY Utica/Rome named tops for Hispanics," *O-D*, December 29, 1996, 3C.

[19]Sonia Martínez, "Dominican Republic Field Study Trip," *Utica Phoenix*, March 2009, 12.

[20]Bill Farrell, "Hamilton College group opposes U.S.-run training school for Latin American soldiers," *O-D*, April 18, 2000, 1B.

[21]Editor, "Latinos' hurricane relief drive applauded," *O-D*, November 4, 1996, 10A.

[22]Crystal Evola, "Foreign-born players help HCCC in nationals," *O-D*, November 9, 1996, 1B.

[23]NJCAA Men's Soccer Records, Updated July 2016, consulted September 17, 2016. http://static.psbin.com/h/b/j4wcj6wtmmhafj/MSoc_record_book_-thru_2015-.pdf.

# CHAPTER 11

[1]Maria Clara, "Viaje hacia futuro/Journey to the future," *O-D*, August 21, 1993, 1B.

[2]Nicole Edwards, "Area's newcomers proud to celebrate the Fourth," *O-D*, July 4, 2000, 1A.

[3]Angel E. Chevrestt, "St. John's conducts first communion ceremony," *O-D*, May 20, 2002, 1B.

[4]Femi Lewis, "Churches smaller but still lead," *O-D*, November 30, 2000, 1-2A.

[5]Mary Frances Manno, "A serene place to pray," *O-D*, July 29, 2001, 1G, 2G.

[6]Lisa Kapps, "Carrying on tradition," *Utica Pennysaver*, March 19, 2009, 1.

[7]Tara Sidor, "A traditional Christmas," *O-D*, December 1995, 4A.

[8]Stephen Szmurlo, "Hispanic community receives Three Kings," *O-D*, January 7, 1996, 1B.

[9]Interview with Tony Colón, March 28, 2011.

[10]Jonas Kover, "Hispanic congregation to share Asbury Church," *O-D*, December 30, 1995, 1C.

[11]*Ibid.*, 4C.

[12]Stephen Szmurlo, "Hispanic group forms," *Observer Dispatch*, January 28, 1996, 1B.

[13]R. Patrick Corbett, "Chancellor Park a melting pot of cultures," *O-D*, July 1, 1997, 1B.

[14]Jorge Hernández, "Nurturing Latino futures," *O-D*, March 4, 1998, 5B.

[15]Jorge Hernández, "Hispanic church rejoices in religious freedom, diversity," *O-D*, November 8, 1998, 1-2G.

[16]*Ibid.*, 2G.

[17]*Ibid.*, 2G.

[18]Kelly Hassett, "Family moved to Rome for better life," *O-D*, July 2, 2000, 10A.

[19]*Ibid.*

[20]Kelly Hassett, "Region's diversity flourishes," *O-D*, December 31, 2000, 8A.

[21]Antonia Cardona, *Te veo luego*, AuthorHouse, 2009.

[22]George Spohr, "Hispanic Christians rally for culture and religion," *O-D*, September 3, 2000, 1C.

# CHAPTER 12

[1]Jorge Hernández, "Finding a Spanish heritage," *O-D*, February 25, 1998, 5B.

[2]Stephanie Scarlett, "Hope brings Hispanics to area," *O-D*, January 31, 1999, 29.

[3]George Spohr, "Latin singer finds comfort zone in Utica," *O-D Weekend Plus*, May 31, 2001, 2.

[4]Cassaundra Baber, "Radio show 'en español' targets Latino community," *O-D*, January 9, 2012.

[5]Adolfo Cova, Superior 95.5 Radio Broadcast, May 25, 2013.

[6]Herb Pinder, "'Frankito' bridges gap for Hispanic community," *op. cit.*, 1B.

[7]Annette Jiménez, "Frank Calaprice helps Utica's Hispanics get things done," *O-D*, December 25, 1990, 3A,4A.

[8]Jorge Hernández, "Utican takes time to help Puerto Rican neighbors," *O-D*, August 10, 1999, 5-6B.

[9]*Ibid.*, 5B.

[10]Aida Di Pasqua, "Puerto Ricans realize American dream in Utica," *O-D*, February 28, 1999, 1D.

[11]Interview with Carmella Edwards, April 2, 2011.

[12] Interview with Mario Colón, December 14, 2009.
[13] *Ibid.*
[14] Erika Irizarry, "Student appreciates Hispanic heritage," *O-D*, November 22, 1997, 6B.
[15] *Ibid.*
[16] Michael Doherty, "New Business: Taino's Restaurant," *O-D*, December 15, 1999, 9A.
[17] Kelly Hassett, "Restaurant fulfills dream," *O-D*, July 3, 2000, 1A, 4A.
[18] Lena Syrd, "The Bronx beats in his heart," *O-D*, April 25, 2002, 1A, 7A.
[19] Shawn Anderson, "Utica Memorial Wall honors diverse group," *O-D*, May 16, 2006, 1-2A.
[20] Interview with Mario Colón, December 14, 2009.
[21] "Obituary Maria Delgado Rivera," *O-D*, February 15, 1990, 7A.
[22] Fabián Ramírez, "Puerto Rico: Isla buscando destino," *O-D*, July 10, 1993.
[23] John Omicinski, "Congress considers offering Puerto Rico statehood in fall," *O-D*, August 13, 1997, 5A.
[24] Valorie Tramm Claburn, "Local residents split on whether Puerto Rico should be state," *O-D*, August 16, 1997, 1B.
[25] Jorge Hernández, "Puerto Rico ponders the American way of life," *O-D*, September 23, 1997, 11A.
[26] Clea Benson, "Puerto Rican voters reject statehood for third time," *O-D*, December 14, 1998, 3A.
[27] Ana Zayas-Withers, "Puerto Ricans are proud U.S. citizens," *O-D*, November 13, 2005, 15A.
[28] Rocco LaDuca, "Spanish eatery battles for liquor license," *O-D*, November 16, 2005, 1B, 4B.
[29] Cassaundra Baber, "New restaurant flavors neighborhood," *O-D*, April 10, 2006, 1B.
[30] Shawn Anderson, "Some say restaurant's name offensive," *O-D*, November 4, 2005, 1B.
[31] *Ibid.*, 1B.
[32] *Ibid.*, 1B.
[33] Interview with Milquiadez Pedro Burdier, September 8, 2010.
[34] *Ibid.*
[35] *Ibid.*
[36] *Ibid.*
[37] *Ibid.*
[38] Cassaundra Baber, *op. cit.*, April 10, 2006, 1B.
[39] *Ibid.*

⁴⁰Cassaundra Baber, "The changing face of a neighborhood," *O-D*, February 19, 2008.

⁴¹Emerson Clarridge, "Flavor of Spanish cuisine comes to downtown Utica," *O-D*, November 20, 2009.

⁴²Cassaundra Baber, "As Dominican population grows, new businesses emerge," *O-D*, February 20, 2011.

⁴³Sara Tracey, "Dominicans keep traditions alive in their new home in Utica," *O-D*, February 23, 2013.

# CHAPTER 13

¹Sonia Martínez, "How the MVLA Was Formed," *Mohawk Valley Latino Association, Inc. Newsletter*, 1:1: Fall-Winter 2006.

²*Ibid.*

³Krista J. Karch, "Latinos organize association," *O-D*, July 11, 2004, 1C.

⁴Cassaundra Baber, "Bienvenidos! Fast-growing Hispanic population celebrates heritage," *O-D*, September 29, 2005, 1A.

⁵*Ibid.*

⁶*Ibid.*

⁷Sonia Martínez, "How the MVLA Was Formed," *op. cit.*, 2.

⁸MVLA, Inc., *Mohawk Valley Latino Association, Inc. Newsletter*, vol. 1, n. 2, Spring-Summer 2007, 4-6.

⁹Chinki Sinha, "Local officials reach out to Latino community," *O-D*, March 29, 2008.

¹⁰Rebecca Croniser, "We want to raise awareness of Latino culture," *O-D*, September 13, 2008.

¹¹Lisa Kapps, "Celebrate local Latino culture during Hispanic Heritage Month," *Utica Pennysaver*, October 2, 2008, 1.

¹²Rebecca Croniser, *op. cit.*

¹³Rebecca Croniser, "Community celebrates Hispanic Heritage Month," *O-D*, October 12, 2008.

¹⁴*Ibid.*

¹⁵Lisa Kapps, "Celebrate cultural diversity at International Festival," *Utica Pennysaver*, April 2, 2009, 1.

# EPILOGUE

¹Earl Shorris, *Latinos. A Biography of the People* (New York: W.W. Norton and Company, 1992).

²Jennifer Leeman, "Categorizing Latinos in the History of the U.S. Census: the Official Racialization of Spanish," in José Del Valle, ed., *A Political History of Spanish. The Making of a Lan-*

*guage* (Cambridge, U.K.: Cambridge University Press, 2015), 305-26.

[3] Claire Mar Molinero, *The Politics of Language in the Spanish-Speaking World* (London: Routledge, 2000), 178.

[4] *op. cit.*, *Sociolinguistic Studies*, Vol. 6, No. 3 (2012), 571-93.

[5] Ingrid Piller, *Linguistic Diversity and Social Justice. An Introduction of Applied Sociolinguistics* (New York: Oxford University Press, 2016).

[6] David W. Chen, "Utica Settles State Claim Alleging Biased Enrollment for Refugee Students," *The New York Times*, July 22, 2016, A22.

[7] Silvina Montrul, *El bilingüismo en el mundo hispanohablante* (New York: Wiley-Blackwell, 2013).

[8] Stacey Van Dahm, "Barrio Art: Telling the Story of Latino Philadelphia Through Murals," *Latino Studies*, Vol. 13 (2015), 421-33.

# INDEX

**A**
Abrams, Erin 32
Abrams, Luis 20
Aguilar, Roque 16
AIDS 47, 68, 69
Allen, Gene 132
Álvarez, Gabriel 90
American Red Cross 114, 127
Andino, Lyvel 125
Aragon, Pepe 114
Arcuri, Jeanne 37
Arcuri, Michael 141, 142
Asamblea de Iglesias Cristianas 92, 118, 149
Asbury United Methodist Church 117
Assaro, Mayor Dominick 16-17
Atayde, Marianyelis 120
Atayde, Martin 120

**B**
Baez, Diogenes 64
Balarezo, Pablo 62-63, 72, 145
Balzano, John 67
Barnum, Pat 20
Barrios, José 34
Basenfelder, C. Fabiola 122, 141
Bassano, Father Mike 23
Basualdo, Sonia 63
Bautista, Jorge 65
Beaunit Mills 39
Belén, Aymmé 141

Belmar, José 48,
Beltrametti, Maria 20
Bendix 26, 29
Bevivino, Mario 80
Bird, Robert W. 117
Blackshear, James 79, 86
Boehlert, Sherwood 109
Bonilla Guzmán, Anibelkys 67, 72
Bonilla-Grasso, Josefina 53
Borrero, Rikchy 64
Bossert Manufacturing 40
Boyer, Mildred 121
Brandegee School 18, 19, 23, 26
Brindisi, Louis 81
Brooks, Annie 86
Brooks, Demetris 86
Brown, Cornelia 67, 70
Brown, Isaac 86
Brown, James 101
Buckley, Judge John 39
Burdier, Milquíadez Pedro 132-135, 156
Bush, George W. 102
Bustabad, Juan 65

**C**
Café Flamboyan 40
Café Tropicano 21, 24, 33, 36, 40
Caffé Caruso 136
Calaprice, Frank 19, 20, 22-23, 27, 38, 123, 124, 145, 148, 150
Calderón, Felipe 122

Candelario, Raúl 119
Cardona, Luis 55, 120
Carretero, Lydia 20
Centro Cívico Hispano-Americano 143
Centro Cívico of Amsterdam, Inc. 143
Chamberlain, Patricia (Pat) 27, 32, 35, 39, 46
Chancellor Park 118
Chaparro, Michael 40
Chavez, David 56
Chavez, Lester 109
Chavez, Tim 55-57, 65, 72, 75, 77, 79, 83, 133, 155
Chicago Pneumatic 91
Clemente, Robert 104
Clinton, Bill 102
Colón, Alma 127
Colón, Anthony (Tony) 66, 72, 105, 116, 128, 138-140, 142, 143, 146, 150, 156
Colón, Luisa 46
Colón, Mario 45, 103, 126, 129, 141, 145, 146, 150, 156
Columbus Elementary School 26, 109
Comité de Dominicanos Unidos de Utica 137
Concepción, Ruth 141
Cortes, Elisa Maria 45
Cortes, Richard 130
Cova, Adolfo 122-123, 146, 149
Critelli, Louis 46
Cruz, Clarissa 20
Cutler, Edward 17

**D**
De Camp, H. Stuart 140
De La Rosa, Carlos Manuel 52
DeJesús, Luis 36
DelValle, Maria Clara 115
DelValle, Rosangie 115
Desmoines, Albert 90
Destito, RoAnn 54-55, 138
DeSuárez, Marilyn 50-51, 54, 74, 76, 78, 90, 102, 150
Diaz, Tabaré 138
Dillon, John 25
Donovan, James 46
Dote, Michael 105
Duffy, Gerald 17
Dybas, Gloria 18

**E**
Eannace, Ralph 102
East Utica Community Center 17-20, 24, 26-30, 32, 34, 40, 124
Echevarria, Pegine 144
Edwards, Carmella 125
Eghigian, Sharon 110
El Barajo Restaurant 11, 134, 142, 149
El Canelo 136
El despertar hispano-americano 53-56, 129
El Rincón Criollo 127
El Toque Final Barbershop 136
Elefante, Rufus 150
Elias, Frank 136, 142
Elsa, Sister 23
Espinal, Maritza 62, 72, 106
Espinal, Sergio 52

Estrada, Jade Esteban 122
*Ethnic Utica* 5
Excellus Blue Cross/Blue Shield 104, 143

**F**
Family Grocery 131
Faro de Luz Seventh Day Adventist Church 149
Feliciano, Linda 70
Fernández, Joseph 47
Ferreira, Zacarías 133
Ficchi, Philomena 123-124
Ficchi, Vincent 123-124
Fitzgerald Culkin, Susan 140
Flanagan, John 22, 25, 34, 42
Foery, Bishop 13
Forett, Mark 136
Foster, Cira 140
Franco, John 73-74, 79-81, 156
Franco, Raúl 65
Franklin Upthegrove Utica Memorial Wall 128

**G**
Gannon, Patrick 59
García, Luis 141
García, Soraida 20, 23
Garramone, Judge Anthony 39
Garro's Pharmacy 136
Gentile, Patricia 19
Gilberti, Jerry 49
Girona, Miguel 17, 23-24
Girona, Nestor 24-25, 27
Gómez, Ramón 26
Gomez, Sylvester "Papito" 136
González, Freddy 136
González, Robert 120
Goya Foods 116, 139
Grant, Deanna 121
Griffiss Air Force Base 11, 26, 44, 52, 90-91, 94
Grimaldi, Lissett 127
Guerrero, Angel 112
Guerrero, Anny 112
Guerrero, Daileny 112
Guerrero, Daily 112
Guida, Amadeo 124
Gutiérrez Luque, Dr. Antonio 17

**H**
Hamilton College 53, 57, 113, 141, 156
Hanley, Lorraine 25
Hanna, Edward 100
Hayes, Michael 76
Haynes, Phillip 142
Heian, Darlene 113
Hendricks, Ron 20
Hendricks, William 52, 101, 112
Herkimer County Community College 65, 104, 114
Hermoso, Rafael 63, 72
Hernández, Jorge 55, 57, 84, 130, 145, 150, 155
Hispanic-American (Spanish) Action League 18, 23, 26-27, 29, 40, 50, 124, 145, 148
*Hispanic Outlook* 113
Hispanics United Buffalo 143
Hispanos Unidos 49-51, 69,

83, 89-90, 105, 139, 146, 148
Historic Old Saint John's 11, 13, 15, 19-20, 22-23, 25, 42, 44, 46-47, 113, 115, 124, 149
Holt, John 85, 87
Holt, Laura 141
Horton, Eugene 20
Hospice Care Inc. 124
Houseknecht, Michael 36

## I

Iberia Foods 116
Ibero-American Action League, Inc. 143
Iglesia de Dios Altísimo 149
Iglesia Maranatha 95, 98, 102, 119, 149
Iglesia Metodista Libre Hispana 117
Iglesias, Julián 135
Iglesias, Lourdes 143
Inoa, Luis 137
Irizarry Santiago, Hilda 16, 29-30, 41, 44, 48, 87
Irizarry Zayas, Anna 50
Irizarry, Amanadab 22, 24, 26-27, 36
Irizarry, Antonio 23
Irizarry, Delia 20, 29
Irizarry, Emilio 14, 50
Irizarry, Erika 127
Irizarry, Gladys 50
Irizarry, Leonor 29, 44
Irizarry, Linda 46
Irizarry, Natividad 23
Irizarry, Nicolás (Nick) 26-27, 29, 40, 44
Irizarry, Norma 20

Irizarry, Philip 23
Irizarry, Rubén 34
Irizarry, Tony 22

## J

Jackson, Ed 104
Jiménez, Ángel 127
Jiménez, Elle 141
Jiménez, Rafael 37, 40-43, 46, 49-50, 146, 150
Joel's Spanish-American Food 131, 140
Johnson, Lyndon 56
Jordan, Hilda 112
Joseph & Feiss 24
Julián's Barbershop 135

## K

Kadic, Azur 86
Kalavazoff, Tania 109
Kelly, Lewis 26
King, Martin Luther 84
King, Yolanda 84
Klein, Barbara 75, 79, 100
Knight, Steven 122
Kokoszki, Linda 70
Kolczynski, John 84
Krzysiak, Casimir 115

## L

La Liga Spanish Action League 67, 143
La Palma Restaurant 29-30, 40
*La Voz de San Juan* 13
LaBella, Nicholas 26
Lackland Airforce Base 122
Lagares, Elving 32
Lagares, William 18
Laino, Nick 80

LaPolla, Mayor Louis 36, 49, 75, 77-80, 82, 86, 100
Laskovski, Pat 20
LAST, 29, 40-47, 49, 124, 146
Latin American Student Union (LASU), 142
Leeman, Jennifer 145
Leingang, Matt 85
López Fretts, Marilu 141
López, Luis 64
López, Maria 130
López, Nydia 130
Lowengard, Daniel 106, 109-110, 112, 130
Lozada, Zuleika 66

**M**

Maldonado, Félix 64
Maldonado, Maria 45
Malte, Julie 137
Mambo's 50
MAMI 66-68, 70-72, 95, 102, 120, 147
Mancuso, Ron 85
Mar-Molinero, Claire 147
Marcy Correctional Facility 10, 96
*Marielitos* 7
Marin, Franklin 133
Marshall, Henry 55
Martin Luther King Jr. Dream Park 128
Martínez, Sonia 65, 104, 113, 123, 135, 137-140, 143, 146, 150, 156
Mathis, David 38
Mattehews, Yelixsa 140
Mattei, Rosalia 65
Mauer, Marc 82

Maye, Cornell 103
McFadden, Jenni 141
McKinsey, Jerome 103
Meier, Raymond 100
Mejías, Legna 85
Meléndez, Alberto 47
Meléndez, Emma 47
Melo, Juan 137
Mendoza, Eduardo 117
Mid-State Correctional Facility 96
Miguel's Body Shop 23
Miranda, Carmen 23
Miranda, Oneida 45
Miss Hispanic Utica 44-45
Miss Latin Utica 44
Missionary Church of Christ 25, 34, 70, 95, 119
Mohawk Correctional Facility 97
Mohawk Valley Latino Organization (MVLA) 6, 67, 104-105, 112, 123, 134-135, 138
Molina, Enrique Irizarry 14
Molina, Franchelis 110
Molina, Santos 12, 21-27, 31, 36, 39-40, 150
Molina, Venera 25
Molina, Virgen 45
Montalvo, Rubén 116-117
Montana, Phil 77, 80
Montoya, Anthony 83, 89
Morales, Edna 116
Morales, Roy 116
Mordue, Norman A. 80

**N**

New Media Party 45
Nick's Place 84

NJ Flihan and Co. 136
Novillo, Jorge 63, 65, 72
Novoa, Sofia 50-51, 150
Nudo, Cristina 65
Núñez, Erik 117
Núñez, Nieve 132

**O**

*Observer-Dispatch* 13-15, 21, 30, 35, 41-43, 50-51, 53-56, 59, 63, 65, 74, 76, 80, 82-83, 88-89, 97, 111, 120, 146, 155
Olguin, Luis 115
Oneida Correctional Facility 90
Oneida Ltd. 122
Ortiz, Juan 131
Ortiz, Erik 12, 73-80, 148, 156
Ortiz, Jeff 40
Ortiz, Nicolás 64
Ortiz, Ralph 23
Osuji, Kenny 118
Otero, Linda 14
Our Saviour Lutheran Church 17

**P**

Padilla, Minerva 143
Pagan, Marian 45
Palmieri, Robert 123
Pamphille, Calvin 128
Party Packing Co. 14
Pataki, George 102
Pawlinga, Steven 26, 36
Peña, Elena 141
Peña, Flerida 141
Peña, Yamil 141
Pérez Alonso, Rev. 120

Pérez, Maritza 95, 98, 102, 119
Pérez, Salvador 54
Perkowski, Anna 20
Pettigrew, Jean 20, 23
Phillips, Bill 132
Picart, Gregorio 40
Picente, Anthony 105
Picente, Eleanor 85
Pilpe, Eduardo 118
Pilpe, Felicidad 118
Pollicove, Allan 39
Polonia, Israel 64
Poplack, Shana 61
Powell, Emily 61
Proctor High School 19, 23, 33, 40, 44, 84-87, 108, 110-111, 113, 118, 125
Proposition 187 73
Puig, Lydia 117

**R**

Ramakrishnan, Devi 85
Ramírez, Fabián 129
Ramos, Robert 44
RCIL 116
Reagan, Ronald 36, 56
Reidy, Robert 59
Reyes, Caridad 70
Ritmo Caribeño 141
Rivera Zayas, Herman 14
Rivera-Sanabria, Félix 67, 72, 147
Rivera, Alejandro 14
Rivera, Elliott 33
Rivera, Hermogenes 129
Rivera, Luis 64
Rivera, María Santa (Delgado) 128, 129, 150
Rivera, Mercedes 46, 49

Rivera, Miguel 23, 29, 30-31, 39-40, 42, 45, 150
Rivera, Miriam 23, 27, 75, 129, 150
Robert, Lee 83
Rodríguez (Sánchez, Cardona), Antonia 15, 25, 70, 95, 119 120, 145, 148-149
Rodríguez, Angelo 133
Rodríguez, Maria del Carmen 69
Rodríguez, Milagros 32, 34-35, 147
Rodríguez, Reynilda 136
Rodríquez, Erlee 85
Rodríquez, Francis 136
Rodríquez, Vladimir 128
Roefaro, Angelo 136
Roefaro, David 136
Rojas, Maria Teresa 70
Román, Carmen 78
Román, Deane 39
Román, Dionisio 39
Román, Gladys 38
Román, Julio 20
Román, Luis 31
Romero, Felipe 121
Romero, Suliema 121
Rosario, Aurea (daughter) 119
Rosario, Aurea (mother) 119
Rosario, Emanuel 119
Rosario, Josue 119
Rosario, Mildred 119
Rosario, Wilfredo 119
Ross, Roberto 43
Roselló, Pedro 130
Rotundo, Benny 102
Ruiz, Caroline 128
Ruiz, Pfendler 101

Ruiz, Ruben 128

S
Saafir, Michael 74-82
Saint Mary's of Mount Carmel 115
Saint Stanislaus Church 12, 23, 115
Salerno, Joseph 115
Salvation Army 118
Sánchez, Juan 78, 89
Sánchez, Presby 120
Santana, Magdalena 18
Santiago, Abraham 33
Santiago, Carmen 35
Santiago, Elsa 33
Santiago, José 50
Santiago, Nelson 39-41, 43, 45, 150
Santos, Jacqueline 118
Santos, Román 62
Sarahman, Melva 101
Scala, Brian 97
Scalise, Bart 76, 80
Scalise, Peter 142
Scalzo, Anthony 19
Schmitz, Theodore 14
Schneider, Penny 18, 37
Schultz, Raymond 39
Scooby Rendering, Inc 105
Shorris, Earl 145
Sims, George 37
Smiegal, Cindy 128
Smith, John 101
Smith, Scott 77, 85
Solete, Marna 63, 145
Soto, Hilaria 132, 135
Soto, Luz 116
Sotomayor, Elizabeth 47
Sotomayor, Luis 47

Spanish Community Center 12, 17, 30
Spanish Community Report 20
Speciale, Harmony 104
Spina, Barry 80
Spraker, Elizabeth 55, 89, 105, 141
St. Francis DeSales 44
St. Mark, Audrey 140
St. Paul's Baptist Church 128
Stanley Performing Arts Center 84
Street Time, Inc. 24, 36
Stronach, Mary 58
SUNY Institute of Technology 26, 70, 113, 118, 141
Superior 95.5 122

**T**
Taino's Restaurant 127
Taylor, Mary 32, 35
Taylor, Tracy Lee 141
*Te veo luego* 120, 149
Techno-Logic Solutions 67, 72, 105
Tejera, Michael 64
The Last Tangle Salon 39
Theodora, Sister 14-15
Tirado, Michael 48-49
Tomer, Susan 15
Torres, Elecuterio 38
Torres, Magda 20
Torres, Sebastian 40
Tri-State Laundries 24
Tropical Delight 136-137, 141
Tu cocina 136
Tudhope, Evelyn 20

**U**
Univisión 65
Unobagha, Zeke 118
Upthegrove, Franklin 17, 128
Utica Academy of Science Charter School 107
Utica Blue Sox 63-64
Utica College 5, 20, 49, 53, 65, 71, 77, 113, 141-142
Utica Common Council 22, 46, 73
Utica Community Action Inc. (UCAi) 13-14, 17-19, 23, 27, 34-36, 38
Utica Free Academy High School 19
Utica Police Department 36-37, 68, 71, 102, 146
Utica United Party 104
V. Ficchi Heating and Air Conditioning Company 124

**V**
Valenti, Jaclyn 87
Valladares, Carlos 31, 33, 35, 36
Valladares, Elvia 31
Valladares, Milton 13-15, 27, 31, 43, 148-150
VanMarter, Shirley 113
Vargas-Rivera, Marline 97, 140
Varona, Grace 141
Velez, Charlotte 36
Ventura, Ruffy 80
Ventura's Restaurant 20, 73, 76, 80
Vera, Erwin 87

Vescera, Frank 142
Vitullo, Florio 36

**W**
Walker, John W. 37
*Wall Street Journal* 57, 86. 148
Wallace, Scott 59
Washington, Diane 92
Webster, Mary 128
Wetmore School 16, 49
Wilmore, Debbie 45

WKTV 20, 24

**Y**
Yacco, Patrick 73-78, 80
Yok Ling 119

**Z**
Zavala, Margarita 122
Zayas-Withers, Ana 131, 133
Zayas, Armando 30
Zecca, Jim 104
Zorilla, Danny 118

BOARD OF DIRECTORS

# THE EUGENE PAUL NASSAR ETHNIC HERITAGE STUDIES CENTER

Juan A. Thomas, Ph.D., Spanish (Director)

John Bartle, Ph.D., Russian

Frank Bergmann, Ph.D., English and German (Director Emeritus)

Sherri Cash, Ph.D., History

John Johnsen, Ph.D., Anthropology

James S. Pula, Ph.D., History (Director Emeritus)

1600 Burrstone Rd., Utica, NY 13502

E-Mail: jathomas@utica.edu

# THE EUGENE PAUL NASSAR ETHNIC HERITAGE STUDIES CENTER

Founded in 1981 by Utica College Professor Eugene P. Nassar, the Ethnic Heritage Studies Center serves as a focal point for research, teaching and public service related to ethnicity in American life. Its objectives are to develop library and other teaching resources in the field of ethnic studies; promote the collection of historical and cultural materials; support the publication of occasional papers, monographs, and other items on topics related to ethnic studies; develop bibliographic references for area libraries, historical societies, and organizations housing research materials on ethnic studies, work with community organizations toward the preservation and dissemination of information on the ethnic experience in central New York; and cooperate with The History Project and the Center for Historical Research sponsored by the Utica College History Department. On April 20, 2011, the name of the Center was changed in honor of its founder.

Recent Publications include (* copies available from the Center): *Essays at Eighty*, Eugene Paul Nassar; *East Utica*, Eugene Paul Nassar; *New York Mills: Evolution of a Village,** Eugene Dziedzic and James S. Pula; *My World, My Time,** Eugene Paul Nassar; *The Graphic Art of Robert Cimbalo*, Eugene Paul Nassar, editor; *With Courage and Honor: Oneida County's Role in the Civil War,** James S. Pula and Cheryl A. Pula, editors; *Rufie: A Political Scrapbook*, Philip Bean and Eugene Nassar, editors; *For Liberty and Justice,** James S. Pula; *La Colonia: Italian Life and Politics in Utica, New York,* Philip A. Bean; *Ethnic Utica,** James S. Pula, editor.

973.046 THO
Thomas, Juan A.
Diary of a small Hispanic community /
$20.00

**EARLVILLE FREE LIBRARY**
4 N. Main St
Earlville NY 13332
(315) 691-5931

Earlville Free Library
0003600700706

Made in the USA
Columbia, SC
29 August 2017